Democratic Education as Inclusion

Democratic Education as Inclusion

Nuraan Davids and Yusef Waghid

LEXINGTON BOOKS
Lanham • Boulder • New York • London

Published by Lexington Books
An imprint of The Rowman & Littlefield Publishing Group, Inc.
4501 Forbes Boulevard, Suite 200, Lanham, Maryland 20706
www.rowman.com

86-90 Paul Street, London EC2A 4NE

Copyright © 2022 by The Rowman & Littlefield Publishing Group, Inc.

All rights reserved. No part of this book may be reproduced in any form or by any electronic or mechanical means, including information storage and retrieval systems, without written permission from the publisher, except by a reviewer who may quote passages in a review.

British Library Cataloguing in Publication Information Available

Library of Congress Cataloging-in-Publication Data Available

ISBN: 978-1-7936-5236-2 (cloth) ISBN: 978-1-7936-5238-6 (paperback)
ISBN: 978-1-7936-5237-9 (electronic)

We can disagree and still love each other unless your disagreement is rooted in my oppression and denial of my humanity and right to exist.
–James Baldwin

Contents

Foreword: The Just Demands of Democratic Inclusion –
Ubuntu Communities and Democratic Education — ix

Preface — xvii

1 Democratic Inclusion/Exclusion: On an Imagined Commensurability — 1

2 Democratic Citizenship Education and Dissensus as Inclusion — 13

3 Race as a Social (Re)Construction of Exclusion — 23

4 Intersectionality, Race and Ethnicity — 35

5 Gender and Citizenship — 45

6 Equality as an Imperative for Democratic Citizenship Education — 57

7 Underrepresentation as a Pervasive Impediment to Democratic Education — 67

8 Why Representation Matters in Teaching and Learning — 77

9 Reopening Debates about Engagement and Belonging — 89

10 Democratic Citizenship Education versus Cosmopolitan Education — 101

References — 107

Index — 117

About the Authors — 125

Foreword

The Just Demands of Democratic Inclusion – Ubuntu *Communities and Democratic Education*

Ronald David Glass

I must begin by thanking Nuraan Davids and Yusef Waghid for the invitation to engage with their provocative analysis of democracy as inclusion and of *ubuntu* as the conceptual and practical guides to the reconstruction of democratic education, and of higher education and PK–12 schooling as well. I am honoured to be asked to address such important topics that have been pressing themselves onto the agendas in nations across the globe, yet I am humbled to be asked to join this conversation within the South African context, a place far from my home. I offer my reflections in heartfelt solidarity, and hope they provide some sustenance in your own journeys towards your freedom dreams of a democratic society founded on equal dignity and respect.

As Davids and Waghid insist, equality is required to enter into the formation of a democratic community and participate ethically in the fraught ongoing negotiations at the borders of myriad inclusions–exclusions; it is required to speak truthfully without fear of the dissensus that makes genuine dialogue, critical understanding and social transformation possible; and it is required if we are all to weave together new possibilities for democratic education and community grounded in *ubuntu*, human dignity and interdependence. I thus ask myself, how can I, never a visitor to the African continent, accept this invitation and enter their reflections from a position of equality, and so I begin with a truth of each as human, as beings on this earth.

I write from my home in Berkeley, California, on unceded lands of the Chochenyo-speaking Muwekma Ohlone peoples, on the great bay that opens through the golden gate headlands to the vast ocean to the west. I grew up a great distance east of here, in the Ohio River valley at the southern reaches of the Algonquian-speaking peoples, in the lands of the Shaawanwaki. My uprooted Jewish and European grandparents arrived in those lands in desperation and hope, fleeing pogroms, imprisonment and orphanhood, and there my own tangled roots got intertwined with the Leni-Lenape people, the traditional grandparents to the Shaawanwaki, who had themselves been driven there by the violence of Christian European colonial powers. There I was born, raised up from the slate clay left behind on the etched glacial scrape that holds the great lakes of North America. As a mud-person I have drawn sustenance from the lands, waters and beings that have since nourished me.

In recognition of these and all our relations as mud-persons and this fundamental equality of existence, I believe we have one starting point for a kind of equality that can guide us through the 'contact zones' – 'social spaces where cultures meet, clash, and grapple with each other, often in contexts of highly asymmetrical relations of power, such as colonialism, slavery, or their aftermaths as they are lived out in many parts of the world today' (Mary Louise Pratt, 1990: 34) – that are the spaces of democratic inclusion. I offer my reflections in the spirit of forging some of the 'transcultural' creativity that Pratt argues can emerge from contact zones, making them also places of new literacies and ways of life, where the reading and writing of words engage critically in the reading and writing of new worlds into existence, as Paulo Freire's work in education as a practice of freedom convincingly demonstrated (2018/1970). Of course, what it is to be human, who counts as human, and whether or not education is permitted to serve its primary aim of humanisation, is precisely part of what is contested within the spaces of inclusion defined by coloniality. So, I begin with not just my humanness but my relation to all other existent beings, and with appreciation for this ineliminable equality of being.

Davids and Waghid consider a number of approaches to democratic inclusion and education and outline their reach and limits. They rightly recognise that inclusion into existing systems and institutions cannot be an adequate basis for equality since those very systems and institutions are both structured by and structuring agents of social, economic, cultural and political domination and its resultant oppression. In fact, the knowledges and practices of schools from the earliest years to the highest rungs of university and the professions, despite their professed aim to develop the full capacity of persons, persistently reproduce both the material orders of superiority–inferiority and the psychological correlates that are necessary to sustain oppression. Thus, even in some of these most open of social spaces, inclusion, insufficient and limited though it is in the effort to extend democracy, yields not the imagined harmony desired by the dominant for their assumed generosity by including the worthy and willing from among the formerly excluded, but an inevitable dissensus.

The limits of inclusion reveal the thickness of the weft into which is woven the warp of power of the cultural threads of the orders of government, labour, church, media, school and language and identity themselves. When one is defined and forced out of the dominant orders, of necessity one is presented with a kind of double bind, and so one must live transgressively, either in the open or surreptitiously (Lugones, 2003). Thus, it is that Davids and Waghid unpack the inclusions and exclusions of racial formation, 'the sociohistorical processes by which racial categories are created, inhabited, transformed' (Omi & Winant, 1994: 55), and they extend their critical analysis to ethnicities and genders. Davids and Waghid make clear that race, class, ethnicity, gender reveal the dominant orders while concealing the human being thus ordered. Even in being named for inclusion, as a race or a gender, for example, one can be excluded in the very 'name' itself since it is a reification of relations of power. For these reasons, even in a context of inclusion, it must be repeatedly asserted that these seeming 'identities' or ideological frames are not some kind of biological truth that somehow tells all that is important to know about a person or people, nor do they tell nothing about a person or people because of their construction – they are not empty and without material realities, and the consequent material realities have both negative and positive attributes. In other words, race, ethnicity and gender each tell about the historico-cultural-political-psychoanalytic processes through which those identities are formed and we experience ourselves, others and the world; that is, they tell about some of the forces that shape our consciousness, our praxis (Glass, 2012).

As Paulo Freire asserts, 'historicity is the starting point' (Freire, 2018/1970) – what makes us human is our situatedness within histories, structures, systems, institutions, languages, meanings, cultures and so on, and these are not of our choosing since we are thrown into them by the accidents of our birth and formation; yet always we are also at the same time making the histories, structures, systems, institutions, languages, meanings, cultures and so forth, of everyday life by the choices we do and do not make, by the practices that we pursue. This understanding, this critical consciousness, enables us to see that race, class, ethnicity, gender and such are indeed *consequences* of domination and the struggles to resist. Now we can understand that the knowledges and truths of the lives of those who are otherwise than the dominant necessarily reveal the truth of the dissensus underlying the seeming consensus of the dominant orders, and underlying the very categories of race, class, ethnicity and gender. As Davids and Waghid underscore, this critical analysis demonstrates the truth of the pervasive intersectional co-construction of the ideological framework of domination and oppression.

Because life is spatially mapped by these lines of power, in our work, in our play, in our love and even in our sleep (just ask the homeless where they can legally repose!), those outside the orders necessarily can only become included where heretofore they must not, should not and cannot be; thus in dominant spaces those who are otherwise move with a DuBois-ian double consciousness (Lugones, 2003). This is why when they speak their truth about diversity, equity and inclusion in these places that now include them, they are so often labelled a 'killjoy' and then blamed as if they somehow caused the fractures and violence of the dissensus hidden in the common sense orders and spaces of our lives (Ahmed, 2017).

Democratic inclusion comes with a cost; diversity and equity work are indeed hard work. The challenges of negotiating and navigating these contact zones have led Indigenous scholars in the Americas to call for a refusal of the legal and institutional recognitions of asymmetrical inclusion built on the foundations of coloniality, and meanwhile they craft new foundations for Indigenous resurgence (Coulthard, 2014) and unweave the narratives of their domination to reveal their *survivance* as peoples and the truth that they never were, never have been and are not now the 'Indians' of the old colonial orders, despite the occupations of their lands and the genocidal campaigns against them (Vizenor, 1994/1999). The creative persistence of Indigenous peoples in sustaining and revitalising their knowledges, cultures and ways of being human has yielded critical interventions not only into the quotidian details of the social and institutional race, class and gender orders, verily the 'human' order of coloniality, but also into the ways that official knowledge production in universities is imbricated within the orders of coloniality which thus requires decolonising methodologies (Smith, 2012) and ethical reorientations for research for justice and community transformation (Glass & Stoudt, 2020), though even these approaches are not without their significant ethical challenges (Glass et al., 2018).

Such reflections lead me to understand and agree with Davids's and Waghid's insistence that equality remains a driving imperative of democratic education even though this entails facing fraught truths of the deep disagreements and conflicts underlying the consensus of coloniality if the present social order is to be re/deconstructed. I also want to reinforce their concern that underrepresentation of formerly excluded members of the society remains an impediment to the required re/deconstruction. No dialogue can happen in absentia. At the same time, there is no question that those who happen to occupy dominant positions in the race, class, gender, religious and so on orders can and must critically interrogate their own formation in both the context of their personal history and their ongoing practices; and to be democratic educators for justice who will facilitate a genuine democratic inclusion, they must make that interrogation public, transparent and accountable (i.e. in simplest terms, they must become ethically responsible). Still, we can see again why Davids and Waghid insist that representation in teaching matters profoundly, just as in every other position of social, cultural, economic, political and religious leadership that shapes the formation of the current and future generations.

It matters who is in the conversation about democratic inclusion and democratic education, and who is in the conversation with the youth who are not only the future of the society but a sizable portion of its present. When a diverse people join together in truth as equals, a re/deconstruction of the old orders can enable each to align with their own community's traditions of resistance to the oppressions that sought to define the totality of daily life, as well as their traditions of renewal and transformation that sustained their survivance; from the strength of these traditions, they can together begin to forge a just democracy. Every community, even the dominant one, has narratives of exemplars that have pushed against domination to open spaces for respectful community, such as whites struggling for black liberation, and men struggling for women's liberation, so there are many rich traditions to nourish new beginnings. As my mentors Myles Horton and Paulo Freire argued, "The more the people become themselves, the better the democracy" (Horton & Freire, 1990: 155), so who is among the people engaged in leading and participating in that social becoming of new generations matters profoundly indeed.

When a diverse people join together in truth as equals, as learners and doers, as beings of praxis, as makers and creators of culture and history even as culture and history are creating them, as human beings, then radical new possibilities can emerge. Critical knowledge production with/in communities can mobilise understandings that suggest previously unforeseen actions that can do the hard slow work of transforming the limits of situations and building a society more aligned with their dreams of justice and freedom, with their hopes for democracy; indeed this difficult work is the very source of a critical hope in antiracism struggle (Glass, 2014). Discovering the power of collaborative learning and the power of learning about power can produce empowered groups that seek to make schools and universities provide a democratic and transformative education for the least advantaged (Oakes & Rogers, 2006), and I believe these efforts also point towards the forms of belonging and engagement that constitute the kind of democratic inclusion and education that Davids and Waghid guide us towards.

As with their critiques of the aims and practices of diversity, equity and inclusion programmes that overlook the core structures of oppression operating within institutions, Davids and Waghid rightly approach cosmopolitan renderings of just democratic communities cautiously. After all, as we have seen already, engaging with one another as full equals, respectfully, is a substantial achievement. Such relations of mutuality cannot simply be willed or declared into existence, and they require the very hard work of trust building and becoming responsible and accountable in our institutional lives, as well as the exceptionally hard work of becoming responsible and accountable in our 'personal' lives, uncovering our own unintended complicities in the dominant orders, our own intersectional complexities and contradictions and our own identity opacities and multiplicities. These 'internal' struggles are as disruptive, painful and transformative, and as much a necessary part of democratic inclusion and education, as the 'external' struggles to re/deconstruct schools and universities, hospitals and courthouses and the public squares of every community. Indeed, these entanglements are precisely why Erich Fromm recognised Paulo Freire's liberatory pedagogy as 'a kind of historico-cultural-political-psychoanalysis' (Freire, 1994: 55), and also why I believe that Davids and Waghid provide a compelling and needed direction for democratic inclusion and education beginning with *ubuntu*, human dignity and interdependence. To demonstrate respect for the equality and dignity of all as a basis of community reveals the need for love in the methodology of the oppressed (Sandoval 2000), a love that emphasises our relationality and the need for compassion for one another, a love that allows us to release ourselves from the certainties of the old orders, including our self-understanding, as we deliberate about our future together and who we might become. Here we might find the grace, flexibility and strength to face the truths in ourselves and others, in our societies and cultures so that we can move with humility and compassion.

Here too we might find the armed love (Freire, 1998: 41) that, with care, makes the just demands of democratic community so that we can become responsible and accountable to one another for connecting our dreams of justice to the shared support and work needed for the transformations in our own selves and in the institutional contexts of our daily lives. This kind of democratic inclusion and education 'unearths seeds of fire' (Adams & Horton, 1975) that can rekindle commitments to the long-haul journey of 'paths made by walking' (Horton & Freire, 1990). As Indigenous scholar Robin Wall Kimmerer reminds us in her meditation on braiding sweetgrass, as we walk these paths, "We should also be looking for *shkitagen*, the ones who hold the spark that cannot be extinguished" (2013: 373). These seeds of fire and sparks that cannot be extinguished insure that those included in creating the just democratic communities that we are hoping for will stay attuned to the equality not just of human being but of all being, and stay attuned to our responsibility to the earth and the generations that abide forever.

I am very grateful that Nuraan Davids and Yusef Waghid close their critical analysis with a return to the natural environment, a return to the earth, water, air and fire that make mud persons of all that slithers, crawls, walks and runs on the earth, all that swims in its waters and flies in its air – here again we find what I believe is the fundamental equality that provides the only genuine possibility for an ethical form of democratic inclusion and education. I hope my own meditations on their generative analysis contribute to the ongoing and urgent dialogues we face in our nations as we reckon with injustice and reach for the promise of pluralistic democratic communities.

REFERENCES

Adams, Frank and Horton, Myles. 1975. *Unearthing Seeds of Fire: The Idea of Highlander*. Winston-Salem, NC: John Blair Publishers.

Ahmed, Sara. 2017. *Living a Feminist Life*. Durham, NC: Duke University Press.

Coulthard, Glen Sean. 2014. R*ed Skin, White Masks: Rejecting the Colonial Politics of Recognition*. Minneapolis, MN: University of Minnesota Press.

Freire, Paulo. 2018/1970. *Pedagogy of the Oppressed* (50th Anniversary Edition). London: Bloomsbury.

Freire, Paulo. 1994. *Pedagogy of Hope*. New York, NY: Continuum.

Freire, Paulo. 1998. *Teachers as Cultural Workers: Letters to Those Who Dare Teach*. Boulder, CO: Westview Press.

Glass, Ronald, D. 2012. "Entendendo raça e racismo: por uma educação racialmente crítica e antiracism" [Understanding race and racism: toward a race-critical anti-racism education], *Revista Brasileira de Estudos Pedagógicos* 93, no. 235: 883–913.

Glass, Ronald, D. 2014. "Critical Hope and Struggles for Justice: An Antidote to Despair for Antiracism Educators." In *Discerning Critical Hope in Educational Practices*, edited by Vivienne Bozalek, Brenda Leibowitz, Ronelle Carolissen, and Megan Boler, 101–112. New York, NY: Routledge.

Glass, Ronald, D., and Stoudt, Brett. 2019. "Collaborative research for justice and multi-issue movement building." *Education Policy Analysis Archives* 27, no. 52. https://www.researchgate.net/deref/http%3A%2F%2Fdx.doi.org%2F10.14507%2Fepaa.27.4470.

Glass, Ronald, D., Morton, Jennifer, M., King, Joyce, E., Krueger-Henney, Patricia, Moses, Michele, S., Sabati, Sheeva, and Richardson, Troy. 2018. "The ethical stakes of collaborative community-based social science research." *Urban Education* 53, no. 4: 503–531.

Horton, Myles and Freire, Paulo. 1990. *We Make the Road by Walking: Conversations on Education and Social Change*. Philadelphia, PA: Temple University Press.

Kimmerer, Robin, W. 2013. *Braiding Sweetgrass: Indigenous Wisdom, Scientific Knowledge, and the Teachings of Plants*. Minneapolis, MN: Milkweed Editions.

Lugones, María. 2003. *Pilgrimages/Peregrinajes: Theorizing Coalition Against Multiple Oppressions*. Lanham, MD: Rowman & Littlefield Publishers.

Oakes, Jeannie and Rogers, John. 2006. *Learning Power: Organizing for Education and Justice*. New York, NY: Teachers College Press.

Omi, Michael and Winant, Howard 1994. *Racial Formation in the United States: From the 1960s to 1990s*. Second Edition. New York, NY: Routledge.

Pratt, Mary Louise. 1991. Arts of the Contact Zone. *Profession*. pp. 33–40. Keynote address, Responsibilities for Literacy conference, Pittsburgh, PA, September 1990. Published by the Modern Language Association, Stable URL: http://www.jstor.org/stable/25595469.

Sandoval, Chela. 2000. *Methodology of the Oppressed*. Minneapolis, MN: University of Minnesota Press.

Smith, Linda Tuhiwai. 2012. *Decolonizing Methodologies: Research and Indigenous Peoples*. Second edition. London: Zed Books.

Vizenor, Gerald. 1994/1999. *Manifest Manners: Narratives of Postindian Survivance*. Lincoln, NE: University of Nebraska Press.

Preface

Discussions, debates and theorising on democratic inclusion are not new; it constitutes a core fibre of the fabric of any democracy and remains under considerable strain given its intersectional weaving into constructions of race, ethnicity, gender, culture, sexuality, class and religion. Inclusion is both the strongest and weakest point of democratic citizenship. If all identity formations can be included, democracy stands to gain the most in terms of its political bearing and principles and what it bodes for the advancement of pluralism, difference, tolerance and peaceful coexistence. The strength of such a society resides in the recognition and inclusion of its heterogeneity; it understands the necessity of using this heterogeneity for the purposes of problem solving and transformation, whether at an institutional or social level.

Recognising and embracing diversity allows us to engage with different perspectives, look at ourselves anew and acknowledge that there is more than one way of seeing and interacting with the world. The greater the diversity, the greater the opportunity to cross over into different life-worlds, and the greater the chance of ridding ourselves of our biased prejudices and our misinformed fears. The greater the diversity, however, the greater the risk of exclusion, and hence, the greater the need for inclusion. At the heart of nearly all debates, and at times, conflicts, is a need or desire for inclusion. This desire cuts across individuals, groups, communities or nationalities and calls from equal rights for women and LGBTQI to the equal recognition of immigrants and all citizens, regardless of race, ethnicity, culture, class or religion. The public sphere has always been a convergence (and perhaps divergence) of identities and hence, competing interests, and continues to struggle in affording equal access, participation and recognition to all identities. Invariably such sociocultural and political developments have continuously sparked a renewed interest in the practice of democratic inclusion.

Most notably, the work of Iris Marion Young (2000) offers a view of inclusion commensurable with notions of communication, democratic deliberation and a recognition of otherness and difference. In this sense, as Young (2000) makes us aware, if inclusion is to bring about democratic transformation, then inclusion has to be understood in relation to solving the ills of democracy. The more a society is able to conceptualise and visualise inclusion, the deeper the entrenchment of democratic ideals (Young, 2000). Concomitantly, the less a society is able to conceptualise and instil inclusion as one of its ideals, the more problematic or thinner the democracy. In this regard, the inclusion of one group might paradoxically imply the exclusion of others or the inclusion of some aspects of an individual or group might depend on their willingness to abandon or repress other aspects of themselves. Black LGBTQI students, for example, might experience inclusion in university residences in terms of their racial identities on the condition that they hide their sexual identities. Hence, Young's (2000) contention that inclusion does not necessarily equate to inclusive processes of recognition, participation or respect; people's external inclusion does not mean that they are included in the internal interplay of power relations. Inclusion in this way becomes a negotiated commodity, which perhaps less explicit than outright racial, ethnic or gender exclusion is not any less harmful. Exclusion is not limited to what is not deemed acceptable or appropriate physically; exclusion extends to the control and prohibition of permissible topics, such as sexuality and politics (Foucault, 1981).

Political and social expectations are often stymied and distorted by individual and communal identities – creating vastly incongruent and unrelated lived experiences, often within the same context. The existence and enactments of diversity continue to present ubiquitous epicentres of misreading, misrecognition and missed opportunities for peaceful coexistence – whether in longstanding or relatively new democracies. As such, the public sphere has never held the same meaning to all individuals or groups and should not have done so. Not only do women access and participate in this space differently from men, but within the category of women, the experiences of black women are unlike that of white women. Similarly, a post-9/11 world has seen rapid entrenchments and delineations between 'acceptable' and 'unacceptable' formations of identities in the public sphere. While unveiled women fit the configuration of liberal democracies, veiled Muslim women do not, for instance.

These regulatory alignments hold profound implications for differentiated experiences of citizenship, between those who occupy the centre of the sphere and those who stand on the margins, between those who are seen, recognised and accepted, and those who are not. The dyadic relationship between inclusion and exclusion is by no means limited to the public sphere or broader conceptions of democratic citizenship. Patterns of differentiation and disparity are as apparent in educational settings as they are in the public sphere. In this regard, there are profound implications for teaching and learning and the life experiences of teachers and learners. Concerns about democratic inclusion, therefore, are as troubling and potentially harmful in the public sphere as they are in educational contexts. In fact, very often, the foundational norms put into place during schooling become the primary determinants of how young people conceive themselves as citizens and how they conceive themselves in relation to others.

Unless young people encounter different life-worlds and perspectives, they are not necessarily prepared or willing to engage with the unfamiliar. It would seem that the more exclusive the educational experience, the narrower the perceptions and perspectives of the teaching and learning. For this reason, we cannot conceive of writing about democratic inclusion in relation to citizenship without affording due attention to the kinds of education and educational contexts, which inform the paradigmatic foundations of inclusion and exclusion in the first place. Teaching citizenship to young people cannot solely rely on external practices and frameworks. Instead, as Biesta, Lawy and Kelly (2009: 8) point out, the teaching of citizenship needs to be supported by deeper understandings of how young people actually learn democratic citizenship through their participation in the communities and practices that make up their everyday lives. They explain that

> [a] focus on young people's citizenship learning in everyday life settings allows for an understanding of the ways in which citizenship learning is situated in the unfolding lives of young people and helps to make clear how these lives are themselves implicated in the wider social, cultural, political and economic order.

It follows that when young people learn about what it means to be a democratic citizen in environments in which they are unlikely to encounter the very diversity which makes democracy necessary, their learning is stifled to a theoretical grasp. Notably missing from this experience is what it means to *be* with diverse beings and thinking – encounters and experiences – which we will argue are critical to understanding the importance of inclusion and the risks of exclusion.

Our concern, therefore, is not limited to what inclusion means but what needs to be questioned and reconsidered in order for exclusion to be disrupted. That is, until we can make sense of and interrogate and bring into disrepute the discursive constructions, which are used as tools for exclusion, democratic inclusion will remain out of reach. From our gleaning of the literature on democratic inclusion, we deduce that practices of inclusion have the potential to be expanded depending on the kind of philosophical lens one uses in expounding on postcolonial, post-critical and poststructuralist understandings of democracy and education. In this context of an ever-evolving scholarship on and about democratic engagement, inclusion and or exclusion, our work acquires significance, specifically, if one considers that our take on democratic inclusion stretches beyond current notions of the practice. In this manuscript, we attempt to do justice to an expanded notion of inclusion through a poststructuralist positioning.

THROUGH A POSTSTRUCTURALIST LENS

It is at the juncture of marginalisation of the other and hegemonic dominance of some that it becomes prudent to re-examine the practice of democratic inclusion. Here we are specifically referring to the paradigmatic way through which poststructuralist thought prompts us to rethink or own conceptualisation of democratic inclusion concerning notions of 'inside' and 'outside'. Poststructuralism, explains Crick (2016),

> represents a set of attitudes and a style of critique that developed in critical response to the growth and identification of the logic of structural relations that underlie social institutions – whether they exist in terms of politics, economics, education, medicine, literature, or the sciences.

Departing from its theoretical object of 'structuralism', poststructuralism can be characterised as an intellectual movement primarily advanced by Nietzsche, who, in turn, influenced notable scholars, including Lyotard, Foucault, Derrida, Deleuze and Kristeva.

In general terms, state Peters and Besley (2017), the conceptual issues underpinning poststructuralism emerged as a series of critiques of structuralism, including its ahistoricism, aculturalism and pseudoscientific status revealing alleged 'universal' structures, whether they be of culture, cognition or language. As such, while poststructuralist writing embodies a style of philosophising, the term should not be used to convey a sense of homogeneity, singularity and unity. It should not, says Crick (2016), 'be thought of as a distinct philosophy that exists separately as its own "structure" – a proposition that would undermine its most fundamental attitudes'.

> Rather, post-structuralism should be thought of as developing or arising only in response to pre-existing structures and, as a set of attitudes, helping us better understand, interpret, and alter our social environment by calling established meanings into question, revealing the points of ambiguity and indeterminacy inherent in any system, rejecting the rationalistic piety that all systems are

internally coherent and circle around an unchanging center, showing how discourses are carriers of power capable of turning us into subjects, and placing upon us the burden of ethical responsibility that accompanies the acceptance of freedom. (Crick, 2016)

For instance, if democratic inclusion has been conceived by many as that practice that creates conditions for engagement, attachment and attunement of some in relation to others, then the possibility exists that the discourse of inclusion and the power relations among humans provoke us to ask different questions about inclusion. One such issue is to rethink inclusion in terms of moving closer together yet paradoxically apart.

Poststructuralism offers opportunities and avenues through which to generate new models of reading, writing and criticism. It pushes us to look and see meanings beyond that which is immediately evident, as manifested actions or practices of democratic inclusion. In many ways, poststructuralism is concerned with what is not there or made visible; instead, it is interested in the margins and the liminalities of lived experiences. The more humans engage and iterate, the more they come to experience one another in their differences and otherness and the more they actually recognise the proximal apartness that coheres them. In other words, people might be democratically included, yet, the closer they get to one another, the more they realise how far apart they actually are. Such a notion of democratic inclusion of moving closer apart and moving further together for that matter invariably offers the practice a different understanding. This is just one example of how we would like to tackle our expanded view of inclusion in which we shall attend to the notion of democratic action vis-à-vis difference and plurality to ascertain what defensible practice of inclusion we can most appropriately conjure up and defend.

STRUCTURE OF THE BOOK

Democratic inclusion is both enacted and contested in and through an array of identity formations and representations – race, ethnicity, gender, culture, class, religion, language, sexuality, among others. As previously discussed, the very constructions and strengths of democratic inclusion are that which destructs it and symbolises its weaknesses. For the purposes of this book, we are interested in representations of race, ethnicity and gender as manifestations of democratic inclusion. Despite the immense theorising of its social fabrication, race continues to operate as a primary determinant of sociopolitical status and access, participation, and inclusion in the public sphere. Moreover, we in agreement with Peters' (2015: 644) contention, that of all disciplines, Western philosophy has seemed most resistant to taking race seriously.

While race guarantees degrees of benefits and privileges to some, it operates as a profound barrier not only in terms of equal inclusion but also in being seen and recognised as an equal human being. Race often operates as a background, yet fundamental determinant of how other identity markers are perceived and ultimately included or not. Here, we are specifically interested in the constructions of ethnicity, which is at times conflated with race and gender, putting into play encrusted hegemonies of othering and exclusion. Depending on the context, ethnicity adopts different forms and social standing – maintaining an external distinctiveness through codified languages, expressions and rituals. Like gender, these forms are fluid and elicit different experiences and perceptions, depending on the context. We observe similar dichotomous constructions in conceptions of gender as we do in that of race. If masculinity suggests strength, power, authority, reason and rationality, femininity is seemingly not any of these characteristics. Instead, women are weak, powerless, devoid of subjectivity and agency, and without reason.

When one precedes gender constructions with racial categories – as in 'white males' and 'black females' you encounter different realms of experiences, different forms of citizenship. The more layered and intersected the individual's identity, the more complex the experience in the public sphere. We know that conceptual understandings of being human and human interactions are profoundly influenced by race. Seemingly, the more we engage on race, as made explicit through critical race theory, the more we come to understand that embedded within racism are intersectional identities, which give rise to increasing forms of discrimination, marginalisation and exclusion – all those aspects of human life that have a direct bearing on democratic citizenship education. When the constructions and interpretations of race, gender and ethnicity are probed, both democratic citizenship and education are brought into scrutiny. In this regard, we know that educational institutions, in particular, 'play a fundamental role in reproducing white privilege and schools are seen as places where racism and stereotypes against ethnic and minority groups take place through a variety of means' (Peters. 2015: 643). Hence, our decision to explore democratic inclusion not only in relation to citizenship but also in relation to education.

The rationale for focusing on race, ethnicity and gender in schools is motivated by two premises. One stems from our agreement with Peters (2015: 644) that of all disciplines, Western philosophy has seemed most resistant to taking race seriously. This is certainly not a new injunction. As Mills (1998: xii) points out in his book *Blackness Visible: Essays on Philosophy and Race*, the 'whiteness' of academic philosophy has long been a source of complaint and wonder to minorities. The second emanates from the idea that if schools were to cultivate democratic citizenship education, the possibility of inclusion and representation could be enhanced. As Bosniak (2006: 1) confirms, citizenship is the common language for expressing 'the highest fulfillment of democratic and egalitarian aspiration'. This seems to be what democratic citizenship education envisages, especially in communities that have previously been subjected to segregation, discrimination and exclusion. However, as we argue for in this book, racial, ethnic and gender concerns might stand a better chance of being adequately addressed if a reconsidered notion of democratic citizenship education were to manifest in schools and their curricula. It might just be that inclusion and representation in schools might be harnessed.

Any book on democracy and inclusion should alert one to what underscores democracy to the extent that it invariably creates spaces for inclusion. Or, alternatively, would it be too cynical on our part to delink democracy from inclusion? Unless what is included does not advance democracy, there is no point in connecting the two concepts. However, if democracy does not include, there is no sense in referring to such a concept as democratic because to include is at the centre of any use of democracy. What is included is not meant to undermine democracy but rather to enhance or even widen the concept of inclusion. We commence this book by examining conceptions of inclusion in the demos and showing how inclusion can either advance democratic actions or not. In other words, we argue that democracy is, first of all, a human action that includes. Second, we show how democracy is widened on the grounds of an inclusion/exclusion nexus. Third, we show how iterations concerning inclusion/exclusion can strengthen democratic action.

We continue by exploring inclusion as paradigmatic and imperative of democratic citizenship. In this sense, democratic citizenship cannot *be* in the absence of inclusion. It is necessary, therefore, to look at what democracy espouses and what it does. Chapter 2, therefore, looks at conceptions of democratic citizenship education, as embedded in notions of the nation-state – meaning that any deliberation on democracy, citizenship and education is necessarily context-bound. Commonly, liberal conceptions of citizenship are conceived concerning three distinct but related dimensions – political, legal and identity, or social. Accompanying and shaping these dimensions are sets of rights and responsibilities, which, theoretically at least, determine the parameters and comforts of belonging. These include legal, ethical, civic, human, political, social, cultural, religious, as well as negative and positive rights. Flowing from these dimensions and their associated rights are a myriad of manifestations of access, participation, belonging, inclusion and recognition – put in place through a contractual relationship between an individual and the state.

Despite the implicit offering of a contractual relationship to all its citizens, it is apparent, within any liberal democracy, that this offering is not on an equal footing to all individuals. Not all individuals or communities can engage with the parameters and provisions of the state as equals. Depending on whom one engages with within the context of a nation-state, the lived experiences of what it means to be a citizen in liberal democracies, or what it meant to be included, exist on an extreme continuum of full enjoyment, to not having any sense of it at all. The kinds of fractured citizenship experienced by a range of individuals and groups in terms of race, ethnicity and gender suggest that the assumption of a universal conception of citizenship, which applies to all people equally, is unsound. In response, we propose a different take on democratic citizenship education: a view of democratic citizenship education that transcends the notion of a contractual relationship between an individual, others and the state. Drawing on Jacques Ranciére (2016), we argue that when individuals exercise their equality, they are no longer dominated and exploited, but they have actually developed the capacity to resist and reject assumptions about themselves and situations. Democratic citizenship based on equality, rather than a contractual agreement, prioritises the autonomy of persons whereby they are summoned to disagree with others in educational encounters. Cultivating equal human relations require more than the contractual arrangement of agreement in the sense that people should be provoked to disagree, and in the pursuit of their dissensus, they would have dealt with dissonance along the way. In this way, democratic inclusion, it is argued, is not just a matter of reaching consensus but that dissensus offers inclusion its ruptured democratic agency.

In chapter 3, we shift our attention to race as a social construction and practice of exclusion. Despite arguments and debates that, conceptually, race is not real, that it is a social construction devoid of any biological and moral significance, race remains a highly visible source of agitation, discrimination and dehumanisation. Arising from this simmering tension is what we understand as relational constructions of 'blackness' and 'whiteness', which, although framed differently depending on the geopolitical contexts, speak to the same grappling not only on race but on the relational tensions between race as a construct and race as a condition of being human. Of course, such a reification of race in itself poses enormous challenges to the practice of democratic inclusion because claims that race is merely invented would put to rest any argument that race should be considered as 'something' that shapes inclusion. Nevertheless, our philosophical take on race itself offers possibilities to rethink democratic inclusion. Likewise, the invisibility ascribed to and owned by 'whiteness' perceivably opens a path of uninterrupted being and thinking. This stands in contradistinction to the lived experiences of 'blackness' where implicit judgements are made before the individual who owns the colour has even spoken.

For democratic citizenship, the dichotomous, at times, oppositional, yet parallel pathways of 'blackness' and 'whiteness' has profound implications. These implications are not limited to states of being; they are on vivid display in who is afforded voice, who is seen, who is recognised, and consequently, who has the power. Similar tensions reside in educational systems and engagements, in terms of who our teachers and academics are and how they present themselves, who our educational leaders are and are presented, what curricula are propagated, and ultimately, what the implications are for democratic citizenship as we continue to sift through prejudicial sub-themes of 'white' competence as opposed to 'black' incompetence. As we wade through the thickness of these debates and tensions, we keep our gaze on the implications for education when race is used as a conditional marker of identity not only in the decisions of teaching but in relation to learning. Equally, when race is used to make pronouncements on teaching and learning, the prejudicial implications for such human encounters are even more devastating and indefensible than looking at race through teaching and learning.

Our focus in chapter 4 is on 'conceptions of intersectionality'. Like conceptions of race, 'blackness', 'whiteness', as well as ethnicity and gender, Kimberlé Crenshaw's 'intersectionality' is not without controversy. Emerging from debates centred on critical race theory, Crenshaw (1989) conceives intersectionality as a prism, confirming the multiplicity of identity and its accompanying perceptions and experiences – whereby the intersectional experience outweighs the sum of racism and sexism. Of key interest to Crenshaw, as it to us, is the need to account for multiple grounds of identity when considering how the social world is constructed and reconstructed. At play here is a theoretical framework through which to consider identity formation and its ensuing multiple points of oppression and discrimination and intersectionality as both methodological and analytical frames and discourses. In this regard, as Yuval-Davis (2011) posits, it becomes necessary that despite the origins of its initial coining, which led to its predominant focus on intersectional minority identities, the concept of intersectionality cannot be limited to the experiences of minority identities or groups. As we argue, there should be as much attention on the intersectional dimensions that form and sustain privilege and the inclination toward discrimination. To this end, our interest in this chapter is to consider the implications for democratic citizenship education when categories of identities and their accompanying social difference are not used as either privileging or marginalising lenses.

Chapter 5 departs from a premise that in a liberal tradition, citizens are presumed to have equal status, rights and responsibilities. Yet, regardless of presumptions of equality that extend into access and participation in the public sphere, citizenship is not without constraints and prejudices – as confirmed by a communitarian interpretation of citizenship. The modern state and its public sphere have long been infused with barricaded constructions of masculinity, which have remained intent upon delineating itself not only from femininity and its accompanying language but any claims to emotion. Women, therefore, have long been relegated to the outside of circles and substructures of society. Despite the purported commitment by liberal democracies to gender equality, the meaning and scope of what it means to engage on an equal basis as a woman continues to be wrapped in dispute.

In this chapter, we draw on a number of theorists, such as Butler (1995), Appiah (2015), and Young's (1989) depiction of oppositional citizenship – that is, one which makes a separation between the universality of the public realm of citizenship and the particularity of private interest. We are especially interested in the dichotomous constructions of masculine-reason as opposed to feminine-emotion and how this opposition or tension serves to support and foment discursively disparate forms of citizenship for women. As such, we provide a critical analysis of universalist conceptions of citizenship, which erroneously conceives citizenship as transcending difference and particularity. We argue that women's democratic rights, social responsibilities and sense of belonging can most appropriately be procured when new possibilities for women's political agency emerge in the realm of citizenship education.

In chapter 6, we show that notions of equality – whether legal, political or moral – have always been at the core of democratic politics. Equality maintains the equilibrium of citizenry – that is, that all human beings enjoy the same levels of equality. To Rancière (2002), for example, equality is not a quality of society; instead, it is a fundamental and inalienable quality of persons and interpersonal relations. As such, he believes that equality is not a goal but a presupposition. Inasmuch as democracy, in turn, presupposes that all its citizens are equal and should be privy to the same set of rights, inequality is an inevitable part of society. On the one hand, society produces and reproduces inequality through its hierarchical structures and hegemonies. In South Africa, notions of inequality were embedded in a dyadic relationship of white superiority and black inferiority. Whites are superior because blacks are inferior; concomitantly, blacks are inferior because of whites' superior stature.

Similar constructions exist concerning gender, religion, sexuality and, of course, class. On the other hand, inequality reproduces itself. Those who are on the receiving end of unequal practices and treatment experience great difficulty disrupting preconstructed norms. It serves the privilege of hegemonies to maintain inequality. Therefore, it follows why Rancière (2002) conceives equality as a quality of the individual rather than society. As such, the individual has the political agency and autonomy to counter inequality (without having to wait on society) and lay claim to equality when this right is being deprived. Although there are multiple notions of equality espoused in liberal democratic theory, we are interested in a notion of equality that can enhance democratic citizenship education. For this reason, we are attracted to Rancière's idea of equality which he couches as equality for recognition (Rancière, 2017: 87). It is such an idea that we examine and explore in relation to democratic citizenship education.

Chapter 7 departs from an acknowledgement that notions of representation are not without criticism. Inevitable questions arise regarding substantive or meaningful, as opposed to symbolic or quota representation. Generally, debates on matters of representation – in terms of gender, race, and ethnicity – are a common centrepiece of liberal democracies. In South Africa, debates on representation are intertwined, at times, subsumed, in agonisms and antagonisms of transformation – locating representation as a desired antithesis of underrepresentation. If one considers Hanna Pitkin's (1967) ideas on representation or representation, it becomes apparent that perhaps the binary construction between representation and underrepresentation might not be as clear and self-explanatory as one might think. On the one hand, necessary questions arise regarding the substantiveness of representation, specifically, as to whether it dispels underrepresentation. On the other hand, what are the risks of attempting to address underrepresentation through representation if what is achieved is framed only in symbolism?

In chapter 8, we contend that the value of cultivating diverse spaces of learning resides not only in engaging with different ways of thinking and being but certainly in widening the scope of learner experience and the capacity to cross over into different perspectives. Moreover, diverse and pluralist educational settings provide both the potential climate and content for learners and students to learn how *to be* with others, as opposed to simply learning *about* others. Comparatively speaking, the same level of attention – certainly not in South Africa – has not been given to the representation of a diverse teaching community in either schools or universities. To us – as will be unpacked in this chapter – the incongruencies that often emerge between learner or student demographics and teacher representation (reflective of society) hold particular implications and consequences for teaching and learning. To this end, we will show that the representation of diverse teaching and learning communities in terms of race, ethnicity and gender – if managed correctly – have the potential to enhance both teaching and learning and cultivate the spaces necessary for constructive dissensus for the purposes of understanding and respect of difference.

In chapter 9, we contend that feeling a sense of belonging can take several forms – from that which is physically manifested and concrete to abstract ways

– and varies from person to person. At times, an individual might have a strong sense of belonging, particularly when their particular values or perspectives are confirmed; other times, feeling a sense of belonging might be under significant strain – leading to an individual feeling disconnected, unseen and misrecognised. Feeling a sense of belonging is critical to the well-being and recognition of individuals, groups, or communities. In educational settings, notions and experiences of belonging adopt added complexities and nuances – which might not be immediately evident to teachers or learners or students. Experiencing a sense of belonging is intricately embedded in what it means to be included – that is, to be drawn into the presence and the presence of others. Inclusion, however, exists in a dyadic relationship with exclusion – that is, inclusion cannot be understood without making sense of that which excludes. Drawing on Jacques Delors' (1996) notion of learning, we offer a different understanding of democratic citizenship education that can contribute to reshaping notions of inclusion, and hence, belonging. In this way, hopefully, we shall respond to racial, ethnic and social exclusions.

We conclude this book by arguing that although there seems to be nothing pernicious about democratic citizenship education, engaging iteratively with others based on exercising one's rights and responsibilities in an atmosphere of coexistence and co-belonging does not necessarily imply that *all* others would be involved. People engaged in enacting democratic citizenship education only do so on account of them sharing a particular space, namely the nation-state. Moving beyond the borders of a nation-state nullifies any act of democratic citizenship education. This is where cosmopolitan education seems to emerge as a viable sociopolitical theory of human interaction. To be a cosmopolitan is not just a matter of being a citizen of the world in the Greek cynic, Diogenes's narrow sense. Rather, being a cosmopolitan implies that one is engaged with all others in the world unconstrained by political borders. In other words, a cosmopolitan being is a stranger to none. Such a view of cosmopolitanism resonates with one that promotes democratic and peaceful relations with others (Held, 2003) as not being a stranger to others implies a willingness to engage with them; and encounter others' ways of living (Waldron, 2000). However, not being a stranger to others also implies that one wants to be known by others and to be interested in their humanity (Nussbaum, 2000). In a way, the kind of cosmopolitan education we advance draws eclectically on human encounters to promote peaceful, democratic engagement accompanied by a recognition of others' own cultural and humane ways of being. If such a view of cosmopolitanism is at play, there is always the possibility to be open to new ways and interpretations about the world without being disloyal to one's own ways of being (Papastephanou, 2015).

Chapter 1

Democratic Inclusion/Exclusion

On an Imagined Commensurability

INTRODUCTION

Any book on democracy and inclusion should alert one to what underscores democracy to the extent that it invariably creates spaces for inclusion. Or, alternatively, would it be too cynical on our part to delink democracy from inclusion? Unless what is included advances democracy, there is no point in connecting the two concepts. However, if democracy does not include, there is no sense in referring to such a concept as democratic because to include is at the centre of any use of democracy. What is included is not meant to undermine democracy but rather to enhance or even widen the concept of inclusion. In this chapter, we examine the notion of democracy and show how inclusion can either advance its actions or not. In other words, we argue that democracy is, first of all, a human action that includes. Second, we show how democracy is widened on the grounds of an inclusion/exclusion nexus. Third, we show how iterations concerning inclusion/exclusion can strengthen democratic action.

THE INTRACTABLE TENSIONS OF INCLUSION/EXCLUSION

Disagreements and debates about inclusion and exclusion have always occupied the public sphere. The question of '[w]ho is in and who is out', states Walzer (1993: 55), is the first question that any political community must answer about itself. This question cuts across political, social and economic domains, including race, ethnicity and gender, and is entirely impacted by context. By necessity, inclusion can only be understood in relation to exclusion. If one individual or group is included, then by implication, another is not. This is the dyadic relationship between inclusion and exclusion – the two concepts are interwoven, and the one cannot be understood in the absence of the other. Moreover, the contextualised nature of inclusion and exclusion means that whoever is included in one context might be excluded in another.

Philosophers, posits Bauböck (2018), have tried to dismiss the problem by adopting one of two contrasting strategies. On the one hand, theorists have maintained that 'democratic principles cannot resolve the problem and therefore we have to accept the historical contingency of political boundaries and the powers of nation-states to determine themselves who their citizens are' (Bauböck, 2018: 3). This strategy, explains Bauböck (2018), reduces the problem to allocating territory and people to states in a way that does not challenge their boundaries and claims to self-determination. On the other hand, the second approach is to stick to a democratic principle and use it to undermine the legitimacy of existing political boundaries. If boundaries are historically contingent, clarifies Bauböck (2018: 4), 'then they do not have deep moral significance and can also be radically questioned for the sake of democratic inclusion'. To Bauböck (2018), the theoretical debate thus seems stuck between positions giving priority either to existing democratic boundaries or to principles of democratic inclusion that potentially challenge all boundaries' legitimacy. To him, this impasse suggests that there is something wrong with the way the debate has been framed.

First, states Bauböck (2018), since inclusion conceptually presupposes an external boundary, a theory of legitimate inclusion claims depends on a theory of legitimate boundaries. Seemingly there is no point, therefore, in arguing for the right of individuals to be included in a particular demos if the legitimacy of that demos itself is either blindly accepted or rejected based on (in)compatibility with legitimate political boundaries (Bauböck, 2018). Second, says Bauböck, questions of boundary and inclusion are among the most contested practical problems in contemporary democratic states – arguably 'a result of democracies becoming more liberal and less self-confident in asserting quasi-natural boundaries of nation, territory and language' (Bauböck, 2018: 5)

To Bauböck (2018), inclusion does not merely refer to crossing a boundary; it also implies a relation of correspondence between an individual or collective claim and an associative purpose. Democratic inclusion 'presupposes agency both on the side of those who are included and those who include them' (Bauböck, 2018: 19). Subsequently, he maintains that there is not a single principle of democratic inclusion but several principles, which includes all affected interests (AAI), all subject to coercion (ASC) and all citizenship stakeholders (ACS). These principles have different roles in relation to democratic boundaries; they are not rivals; they complement each other because they serve distinct purposes of democratic inclusion (Bauböck, 2018: 6). To Bauböck (2018: 27–28), 'AAI refers specifically to interests in policy *decisions* rather than to interests in rights protection by *government* institutions or to *membership* in a political community'. The ASC principle 'captures the idea that the democratic legitimacy of government coercion depends on securing equal liberties for all whose autonomy it restricts' (Bauböck, 2018: 28). Unlike the AAI principle, the ASC principle distinguishes between those who are subject to government coercion and those who are not, and it attributes special inclusion claims to the former only. In other words, not everyone whose interests are affected is subjected to coercion (Bauböck, 2018).

The ACS principle is based on a recognition of humans as social beings, who, according to Bauböck (2018: 40), 'have strong stakes [in membership] in being recognized as members of particular political communities because being an outsider who does not belong to any such community is a condition of extreme precariousness'. Stated differently, '[c]itizens are stakeholders in a democratic political community insofar as their autonomy and well-being depend not only on being recognized as a member in a particular polity, but also on that polity being governed democratically' (Bauböck, 2018: 40). In this regard, explains Bauböck (2018), 'Unlike AAI and ASC, ACS derives inclusion claims from a correspondence between individuals' interests in autonomy and well-being and the collective interests of all citizens in their polity's self-government and flourishing'.

Although Kymlicka and Donaldson (2018) are in broad agreement with Bauböck's (2018) general argument for a recognition of multiple principles of democratic inclusion tied to multiple types of polity, they are concerned about a range of cases that fall outside of normal assumptions about who is eligible for, or capable of, citizenship – that is, those who lack the capacity to engage in the kind of rational deliberation about political propositions that are widely assumed to characterise democratic citizenship. As far as Bauböck (2018) is concerned, membership in the demos is not a right of social membership, but a privilege restricted to those who possess certain sophisticated cognitive capacities (linguistic agents) for rational deliberation – known as a 'capacity contract' (Kymlicka & Donaldson, 2018). To Kymlicka and Donaldson (2018: 161), however, some cases involve children, people who have cognitive disabilities, immigrants, as well as domesticated animals, who 'raise a fundamental challenge to our theories of democratic inclusion, not just about who is included, but also about what it means to be a citizen and how to characterize the underlying moral purposes of citizenship'. They contend that citizenship is not ultimately about being affected by particular decisions or being subject to particular laws, 'but about *membership* in a self-governing society. In short, citizenship should track social membership' (Kymlicka & Donaldson, 2018: 165) – explained as follows:

We can call this the membership model of citizenship, which ties citizenship to an ethos of membership. To be a citizen is to be a member of the society (or 'the public' or 'the people') in whose name the state governs, and one central function of citizenship is precisely to acknowledge this membership, to acknowledge who belongs here, who has made a life here, and who therefore has a right to shape the terms of our shared social life. . . . [W]e make a life for ourselves in a particular society, develop social ties within that society, and our well-being is pervasively tied up with the shared norms that govern the scheme of social cooperation, and with how we are treated by our fellow members. Citizenship is an acknowledgement of this 'stake in membership': it affirms that we are members of this intergenerational community, and that, as such, we have a right to shape its social norms and to co-author its laws, as well as a responsibility for its long-term future.

It is Kymlicka and Donaldson's (2018: 176) argument that a truly democratic society would seek to support the political agency of all its members, rather than finding ad hoc or arbitrary thresholds to empower some and exclude others. To them, a 'capacity contract' is not only arbitrary but also generates politically pernicious myths and prejudices (Kymlicka & Donaldson, 2018: 176). In this sense, the contributions of children, people with cognitive disabilities and immigrants are trivialised; they are seen as burdensome. As such, continues Kymlicka and Donaldson (2018: 176–177), 'the commitment to exclude or segregate certain members from citizenship generates cognitive pressure to redescribe their exclusion as a beneficial form of pastoral care and protection, ignoring the realities of burdens, harms and subjugation'. In sum, while the membership model states that individuals are owed citizenship by virtue of their participation in schemes of social cooperation that are subject to collective governance, defenders of the capacity contract tend to trivialize the extent to which children, people with cognitive disabilities and domesticated animals are subject to power or engage in contribution (Kymlicka & Donaldson, 2018).

The insightful analyses of the tensions which beset democratic inclusion by Bauböck (2018) and Kymlicka and Donaldson (2018) provide a rich sounding-board for our ensuing discussion, as well as the rest of this book. Not only is democratic inclusion multidimensional and experienced differently in relation to its polity, but the richer or wider the diversity of a society, the deeper the risks of (social, political, economic) exclusion. Hence, Goodin's (1996: 343) contention that the true source of our anxieties lies not in the practice of exclusion but in that of inclusion. To Goodin (1996: 344), the problem of exclusion

> is that there *is* an inclusive community, be it catchment broad or narrow. And if *that* is the problem, then the solution is not to make our communities more

inclusive but rather to change their nature – making them at one and the same time both less exclusive and less inclusive.

Built into the very logic of both inclusion and exclusion, explains Goodin (1996), is a focus on marginality, margins and boundaries. In this regard, an individual is either 'kept in' or 'kept out', and what 'keep[s] them out', says Goodin (1996: 347), is necessarily defined in terms of the boundaries that delimit 'inside' from 'outside'. Concepts, such as inclusion and exclusion, are defined in relation to what they are not – that is, there can be no inclusion if there is no exclusion. Inclusion, therefore, implies exclusion; and exclusion implies inclusion (Goodin, 1996).

There is, of course, as Goodin (1996) reminds us, another perspective – one that constructs exclusion to infer exclusivity. Referring to 'exclusivity' rather than 'exclusion', explains Goodin (1996), seems to shift the focus away from the margins and what qualities are being filtered out and towards the core and the qualities that are characteristically found within. The outcome, however, remains the same: some are in, and others are not. Following Goodin (1996: 348), exclusivity is characteristically constructed not by who is allowed in but instead by who is kept out. To Goodin (1996), the language of politics, as encountered in the points and debates offered by Bauböck (2018) and Kymlicka and Donaldson (2018), is no different to the ordinary language lived in daily experiences. 'Far from moving us beyond marginality – far from helping to take "the excluded" to the centre life – political appeals couched in terms of "inclusion of the excluded" only succeed in pushing them "just over the line"' (Goodin, 1996: 348). Goodin's (1996: 348) biggest concern is that framing the argument in terms of 'inclusion of the excluded' constitutes an argument for 'just over' the line; certain categories or groups of people remain borderline. As long as they are on the 'right side' of the line, asserts Goodin (1996: 384), 'there is nothing in this language, logic standing behind it, that would help us address our larger about social marginality'. In echoing a similar concern as Goodin (1996), Graham and Slee (2008: 280) reason that the question is not so much how we move '*toward* inclusion', but rather what we need to do in order to disrupt the construction of the centre from which exclusion derives.

DEMOCRACY, INCLUSION AND SHARED COMMON INTERESTS

For more than a century, democracy has been associated with human actions that are participatory, representative and deliberative. When John Dewey (1925) produced his monumental text *Democracy and Education*, he envisaged a form of education as social action that 'occurs by means of communication of habits of doing, thinking, and feeling from the older to the younger' (Dewey, 1925: 3). It is not so much that the older generation always inspires the younger but more that humans of various generations 'live in community in virtue of the things they have in common' (Dewey, 1925: 5). These commonalities, like aims, beliefs, aspirations and shared knowledge, are ensured based on communication, which Dewey refers to as education. To Bauböck (2018), democracy would be unnecessary in the absence of diversity of interests, identities and ideas. Democracy, according to Bauböck (2018: 8), 'is a system of political rule that provides legitimacy for collectively binding decisions and coercive government under conditions of deep and persistent diversity'. Concomitantly, 'political ideologies that consider diversity as a nonideal condition to be overcome through a transformation of society are, therefore, always potentially hostile toward democracy' (Bauböck, 2018: 8).

What education does, following Dewey (1925: 12), is to cultivate processes of continual reorganising, reconstructing and transforming so that these diverse interests are brought into a space of public deliberation and public good. Thus, for Dewey (1925: 100), education has two elements that point towards democracy: first, to have shared common interests on the basis of which humans engage socially and, second, to interact freely among one another through a process of continuous readjustment constitutes what it means to engage in democratic education. As noted by McLaughlin (1992: 236), while

> the identity conferred on an individual by citizenship is seen mainly in formal, legal, juridical terms . . . the citizen must have a consciousness of him or herself as a member of a living community with a shared democratic culture involving obligations and responsibilities as well as rights, a sense of the common good, fraternity, and so on.

The idea of shared common interests pertains to that which binds us and enhances us in our collective humanity.

What follows from such a Deweyan notion of democratic education is that humans engage in and about shared common interests. Moreover, for them to share common interests implies that they are recognised as humans for the interests they advocate. When humans do so freely, that is, without being constrained by this or that, their engagement occurs unhinderedly on the basis of which they can reorganise, reconstruct or transform the educative process. It is not only that they are included in the engagement but also that collectively (democratically) can alter or transform the educative process with others. Young (2000: 52) advances a similar argument when she describes inclusion as a normative ideal of democracy in which citizens can participate in political deliberations, and 'make proposals and criticize one another, and aim to persuade one another of the best solution to collective problems'. As such, '[i]nclusion increases the chances that those who make proposals will transform their positions from an initial self-regarding stance to a more objective appeal to justice, because they must listen to others with differing positions to whom they are also answerable' (Young, 2000: 52). To Young (2000: 12), it follows that when individuals listen, critically engage with each other in an inclusive process, and are willing to reconsider initially held beliefs, they can better resolve inequalities and work towards justice.

In contrast, when humans are misrecognised and not considered as beings who can alter the educative process, it can be inferred that they would be excluded. As Taylor (1994: 25) explains,

> [O]ur identity is partly shaped by recognition or its absence, often by the misrecognition of others, and so a person or group of people can suffer real damage, real distortion, if the people or society around them mirror back to them a confining or demeaning or contemptible picture of themselves. Nonrecognition or misrecognition can inflict harm, can be a form of oppression, imprisoning someone in a false, distorted, and reduced mode of being.

Identity, explains Taylor (1994: 33), is who we are, where we have come from and serves as the background to our interests, our values, our tastes, our opinions, as well as our aspirations. Identity provides us with our distinctive humanity. To Taylor (1994: 30), '[t]here is a certain way of being human that is my way'. Humans can only live their lives in a way they have come to understand; their identity, how they conceive themselves, is what gives shape to their unique identities. When they are prevented from being true to who they are – through misrecognition or discrimination – they miss being what being human is for them (Taylor, 1994). Waghid (2011: 31) describes this as disrespecting the life-world of others and maintains that '[t]he point about respecting the life-world of others is that it involves experiencing them as they present themselves and not fitting into some kind of preconceived picture of one's own imaginings – that is, what others should be like'. In other words, on the grounds of exclusion, humans would not be recognised for the common interests to adjust and reorganise the educative process. They would be excluded. Thus, democratic inclusion for Dewey (1925) involves at least three moments, namely, that they share their common interests, engage unconstrainedly and enact their capacities to alter the educative process.

Now that we have given some account of unhindered democratic inclusion, next we move on to a discussion of democratic inclusion according to Jacques Derrida's views.

DEMOCRATIC INCLUSION AND BECOMING

Whereas Dewey connects democracy to the cultivation of shared common interests, Jacques Derrida links democracy to enhancing human responsibility (2004: 15). Notably, Derrida seldom used or understood democracy to infer a particular form of government. Instead, to him, it embodied a political culture comprised of rights, equality, freedom of expression and the inclusion of minorities. Therefore, to act responsibly within a democracy is to propose and play off one risk against another, such as when humans exercise a suspicion towards matters of public concern (Derrida, 2004: 150). Thus, humans in pursuit of democratic action are always in the process of reappropriating their interests according to certain historical, techno-economic, politico-institutional and linguistic conditions (Derrida, 2004: 151). As the sociopolitical conditions are changed, humans' actions become more democratic when they engage in vigilant actions to ensure greater responsibility. Moreover, acting responsibly requires that humans go beyond the profound – that is, a step further towards 'the chance of an event about which one does not know whether or not' it will manifest (Derrida, 2004: 154). In this way, democratic action is not only risky but also a pursuit towards that which is not yet and which might not be. In other words, taking up a democratic responsibility is to pursue actions 'of what is not yet' (Derrida, 2004: 355).

This argument is reflective of his articulation as 'democracy to come'. It is an acknowledgement that the promise of democracy might not be fulfilled, and yet, an appeal not to lose faith in it. Derrida connects democratic action to responsibility towards 'the strange destiny' of what can still happen in retaining the hope. What one infers from such a notion of democratic action is that when humans do things together, they are not merely governed by an association of beings in constant reflection but also when they reflect about social matters they do so with an openness to the unexpected, the contradictions, conflicts and differences they would be confronted with. Their desire for 'organic union' – that is democratic action or inclusion – is stimulated by a discourse of common autonomy and agency through which their thinking towards renewal is both a desire for memory and exposure to the future (Derrida, 2004: 154). Thus, following Derrida, democratic (inclusive) action is not a matter of bringing humans together only but that their collective action is geared towards a responsibility towards the possibility of chance.

Democratic inclusion does not only involve humans exercising their professional rigour and competence concerning what is 'inside' of the process of engagement but also concerning what is not there, that is, towards the 'outside' (Derrida, 2004: 150). Moreover, when humans envisage transforming their actions such as modes of writing, pedagogy or procedures of academic exchange in relation to their discipline, they venture onto a path that allows them to go as far as possible – towards the 'outside' (Derrida, 2004: 150). In other words, democratic engagement is not just about looking at the inside to those included but also towards the outside where the excluded might open up some possibilities towards seeing the improbable. By implication, democratic inclusion does not seem to be plausible only because it recognises the insiders but also because it makes humans aware of what outsiders might contribute to the future that is still to come. In this way, democratic inclusion seems to provoke insiders to connect with outsiders or what the outside might yet reveal. This leads us to proffer that democratic exclusion is equally necessary for the process of human engagement. If not, we would intentionally misrecognise what the outside might still offer the engagement or how democratic action might yet be awakened in dealing with the strange and other.

Thus, what we have been arguing is that democratic inclusion is not only about engaging with shared common interests. Instead, it also points towards risky human action, which plays off risks as people endeavour to make sense of what remains 'outside' of their educative ventures. Consequently, it does not seem odd to make a case for acting responsibly towards democratic exclusion as well. Next, we examine how far democratic inclusion/exclusion can take us in enhancing democratic action.

ON ITERATIONS AND DEMOCRATIC INCLUSION/ EXCLUSION: AN IMAGINED COMMENSURABILITY?

We have now made an argument in defence of democratic inclusion/exclusion. However, at face value, it might seem as if the two concepts are mutually exclusive entities. We hold a different view. Inclusion and exclusion are relational in the sense of what is inside of practice are connected to what happens outside of it and vice versa so that inclusion–exclusion exists as a singular concept. Therefore, in this section of the chapter, we show how democratic iterations, as developed by Seyla Benhabib (2011), can further enhance the interrelationship between democratic inclusion and exclusion. Democratic iterations, explains Benhabib (2004: 179), are 'those complex processes of public argument, deliberation and exchange through which universalist rights claims are contested and contextualized, invoked and revoked, posited and repositioned, throughout legal and political institutions, as well as in the associations of civil society'. In the process of repeating a term or a concept, she explains, we never simply produce a replica of the first original usage and its intended meaning. 'Through such iterative acts a democratic people which considers itself bound by certain guiding norms and principles reappropriates and reinterprets these, thus showing itself to be not only the *subject* but also the *author of the laws*' (Benhabib, 2007: 454).

According to Benhabib (2011: 151–152), democratic iterations occur in overlapping communities of conversation concerning questions of moral, political and constitutional commitments of people. More specifically, such communities embark on public self-reflection and defensiveness on the grounds that they proffer justifiable accounts of their claims (Behabib, 2011). Yet, what is significant about the deliberative conversations of such communities is that they do not just talk with one another on the basis of argumentation and debate; they talk back in the sense that they critically question the authenticity of one another's arguments in a spirit of openness and democratic legitimacy (Benhabib, 2011).

It is the practice of democratic iterations – that is, people repeatedly talking back to one another – that can bridge an apparent divide between democratic inclusion and exclusion. Through democratic iterations, humans engage in public argument, deliberation and exchange through which claims of universalist rights are contested and contextualised, invoked and revoked in the associations of civil society (Benhabib, 2011: 16). To Benhabib (2011: 129), '[e]very iteration transforms meaning, adds to it, enriches it in ever so subtle ways . . . [e]very act of iteration involves making sense'. Interestingly, an iteration extends into a realm of the unknown whereby humans are summoned to engage in public deliberation even if they are not included in a physical relation of proximity. That is, humans outside of the iterative process can be encouraged to be involved and 'initiate action and opinion to be shared by others [inside]' (Benhabib, 2011: 129). Hence, democratic iterations seem to bring the inside into deliberation with what seems to be outside. This implies that democratic iterations bridge a public conversation according to which humans can 'judge as legitimate or illegitimate processes of opinion and will-formation' (Benhabib, 2011: 130). In this regard, she is clear that democratic iterations are not concerned with the question, 'Which norms are valid for human beings at all times and in all places?' (Benhabib, 2007: 455). Instead, the concern is with questions such as the following: 'In view of our moral, political and constitutional commitments as a people, our international obligations to human rights treaties and documents, what collective decisions can we reach which would be deemed both just and legitimate?' (Benhabib, 2007: 455). To this end, the aim of democratic iterations is that of democratic justice.

What follows from the aforementioned argument is that democratic inclusion and exclusion do not have to be seen as mutually independent entities. They are overlapping moments of democratic iterations in terms of which humans can be included and excluded simultaneously and on the grounds of which their thoughts and justifications can be iteratively (re)considered. We contend that such an imagined commensurability between democratic inclusion and exclusion holds the potential for greater representation and legitimacy as far as human encounters are concerned.

In concluding this chapter, inclusion and exclusion do not exist independently of each other. These practices are mutually intertwined in the sense that if it is more included, humans by implication would be less excluded. Conversely, if it is more excluded, humans would enjoy less inclusion. However, although humans might be subjected to more inclusion and less exclusion or, alternatively, more exclusion and less inclusion, they are not entirely excluded or included. Our argument for such a nexus of inclusion/exclusion is merely to accentuate the degree of inclusion and/or exclusion humans might encounter. The point is, when inclusion/exclusion are considered democratically, the interrelationship between the two practices is either tilted more to inclusion or more to exclusion.

Chapter 2

Democratic Citizenship Education and Dissensus as Inclusion

INTRODUCTION

In this chapter, we explore conceptions of democratic citizenship education, as embedded in notions of the nation-state – meaning that any deliberation on democracy, citizenship and education is necessarily context-bound. Commonly, liberal conceptions of citizenship are conceived in relation to three distinct but related dimensions – political, legal and identity, or social. Accompanying and shaping these dimensions are sets of rights and responsibilities, which, theoretically at least, determine the parameters and comforts of belonging. These include legal, ethical, civic, human, political, social, cultural, religious, as well as negative and positive rights. Flowing from these dimensions and their associated rights are a myriad of manifestations of access, participation, belonging, inclusion and recognition – put in place through a contractual relationship between an individual and the state.

Despite the implicit offering of a contractual relationship (a 'capacity contract') to all its citizens, it is apparent, within any liberal democracy, that this offering is not on an equal footing to all individuals. Not all individuals or communities are able to engage within the parameters and provisions of the state as equals. Depending on whom one engages with within the context of a nation-state, the lived experiences of what it means to be a citizen in liberal democracies, or what it meant to be included, exists on an extreme continuum of full enjoyment, to not having any sense of it at all. The kinds of fractured citizenship experienced by a range of individuals and groups – in terms of race, ethnicity and gender – suggests that the assumption of a universal conception of citizenship, which applies to all people equally, is unsound. In response, we propose a different take on democratic citizenship education: a view of democratic citizenship education that transcends the notion of a contractual relationship between an individual, others and the state. Drawing on JacquesRanciére (2016), we argue that when individuals exercise their equality they are no longer dominated and exploited but they have actually developed the capacity to resist and reject assumptions about themselves and situations. Democratic citizenship based on equality, rather than a contractual agreement, prioritises the autonomy of persons whereby they are summoned to disagree with others in educational encounters. Cultivating equal human relations require more than the contractual arrangement of agreement in the sense that people should be provoked to disagree, and in the pursuit of their dissensus, they would have dealt with dissonance along the way. In this way, democratic inclusion, it is argued, is not just a matter of reaching consensus but that dissensus offers inclusion its ruptured democratic agency.

CITIZENSHIP: THE GOOD(S)

It is worthwhile to start a discussion on citizenship by turning to the ideas of T. H. Marshall (1950). In defining citizenship as a status bestowed on the full members of a community, Marshall (1950) differentiates between three intertwined parts of citizenship: civil, political and social. The civil component comprises the rights required for individual freedom, such as personal liberty, freedom of speech, right to own property, freedom of thought and the right to choose one's own occupation (Marshall, 1950). While the political element refers to the right to participate in the exercise of political power, such as voting, the social element infers the right to live in peace, with access to economic welfare. Much, of course, has changed since Marshall's (1950) proposal, with Benhabib (2005) suggesting that that the concept of citizenship in the modern state can be analytically divided into three components: the collective identity of citizens along the lines of shared language, religion, ethnicity, common history and memories; the privileges of political membership in the sense of access to the rights of public autonomy; and the entitlement to social rights and privileges. Flowing from these dimensions and their associated rights are a myriad of manifestations of access, participation, belonging, inclusion and recognition.

Whether explicit or implicit, conceptions of citizenship suggest 'a contractual relationship between the person and the state' (Yuval-Davis, 2011), which, on the one hand, secures the rights of the individual and, on the other hand, allows the state to enact its laws and policies. Stated differently, an individual surrenders some of his or her personal freedom to the nation-state and, in return, the individual can expect the civil freedom to think and act rationally and morally, while living in peace, free from harm and oppression (Locke, 2003; Rawls, 1971). As such, seemingly – in modern-day liberal democracies – the relationship between the state and the citizens is utilised for mutual preservation purposes. Citizenship, therefore, relies on a mutual contingency between the state and its citizens – in terms of understanding the practices and conduct of citizenship in relation to the state, being capacitated and willing to actively participate in the expectations and norms of the state, as well as not acting contrary to the conditions and laws of the state – hence, the importance of citizenship education.

Good citizens, explains Levinson (2010: 317),

> may be those who vote, protest, boycott, run for office, join political parties, join civic organizations, commit acts of civil disobedience, circulate e-mail petitions, write influential political blogs, 'tweet' or text message about political events being kept under a news blackout, and attend neighborhood council meetings.

Good citizens, she continues, are not only personally responsible citizens but are participatory and justice-oriented. They might disagree, says Levinson (2010), about the productive or effective actions to take as citizens, and they might also disagree about the best approaches to citizenship education. However, they both embrace the importance of knowledgeable, skilful, active involvement in civic and political institutions in order to improve society. Modern liberal democracies, therefore, argues Benhabib (2004: 2), owe their stability and relative success to the coming together of two ideals that originate in distinct historical periods: the ideal of self-governance, which defines freedom as the rule of law among a community of equals who are 'citizens' of the polis, and who thus have the right to rule and to be ruled.

Such thinking informs Gutmann's (1999) argument, which maintains that at the core of civic education is the idea of 'conscious social reproduction'. She asserts that conscious social reproduction consists of knowledge about the political institutions and processes that make liberal democratic institutions possible. It comprises the dispositions and attitudes necessary for the participation and maintenance of modes of governance and the critiquing of such modes. To participate in and deliberate on complex political and social matters, Gutmann (1999) explains that citizens need to develop a capacity for moral reasoning and critical self-consciousness. Inasmuch, therefore, as the modern nation-state needs an educated citizenry to evolve and flourish, so too, citizens are in need of the amenities, infrastructure, opportunities and clean governance for the benefit of individual thriving, in turn, the public good. In the words of Gutmann (1999: 42),

> [a] democratic state is therefore committed to allocating educational authority in such a way as to provide its members with an education adequate to participating in democratic politics, to choosing among (a limited range of) good lives,

and to sharing in the several subcommunities, such as families, that impart identity to the lives of its citizens.

CITIZENSHIP: THE BAD AND THE UGLY

It seems apposite to follow a discussion on Marshall's (1950) definition of citizenship as 'full members of a community', with one which draws on Roche (1987). The liberal tradition, states Roche (1987), presumes that all citizens enjoy equal status, equal rights and duties; principles of inequality deriving from gender, ethnic or class are not supposed to be relevant to the status of citizenship. When citizens agree to abide by a particular framework of citizenship, they presume to share a common set of expectations not only with others but with the state. The idea, therefore, of entering into a contractual relationship with the state is an appealing and desirous one, given what it offers in return in terms of access to a set of rights – whether human, legal or civil. It is easy to understand the inherent problems that might arise from particular suppositions – such as the expectation of a preparedness to engage with the state in terms of upholding its mandate.

Despite the implicit offering of a contractual relationship to all its citizens, it is apparent, within any liberal democracy, that this offering is not on an equal footing to all individuals. Not all individuals or communities are able to engage with the parameters and provisions of the state as equals. Group differences, states Banks (2008: 4), are not included in a universal conception of citizenship – particularly concerning women and 'people of colour'. While there might be a widespread agreement with T. H. Marshall's (195) conception of citizenship as 'full membership in a community', not all citizens would, in fact, be afforded this right (social, political or civil). The assumption, therefore, that there is a universal conception of citizenship that applies to all people equally and that transcends particularity and difference is, in fact, flawed (Young, 1989).

As Levinson (2010: 317) asserts, the idea of a 'good citizen', as described earlier in this chapter,

> arguably privileges traditional modes of civic action that are both increasingly outdated and unrepresentative of a range of actions and behaviours that have historically been important civic tools of members of disadvantaged, oppressed, or marginalized groups or any combination of the three.

Some stand within what is described as the beneficial circle (White, 1999), and are able to contribute to the strengthening of their societal democracy, and strengthen the bonds of their community and society through their education, their work, their charity or activism. Others, however, stand on the outside, falling into the ambit of the welfare category, waiting for the contractual relationship to alleviate their plight. Unlike the former group who uphold the contract because they live by the benefits of the contract, those who exist outside of the circle seldom experience, feel or understand the discourse of their own citizenship in relation to the state. This is not to say that they do not see it – indeed they do – but their citizenship remains trapped in that of witnessing, of peripheral anticipation, rather than living. The impending polarisation and disillusionment, which arise from a peripheral existence, are increasingly ubiquitous across liberal democracies, regardless of geopolitical contexts. To Gutmann (in an interview with Sardoc, 2018: 248), the increasing economic and social divide in and across societies is the most pressing problem facing education for citizenship and individual well-being more generally.

The experience of peripheral citizenship is not limited to poor or disenfranchised individuals or communities. Often, the indigenous people of a state are not only the most marginalised and neglected but also the poorest, which could, of course, provide some explanation for their marginalisation in the first place. There are degrees of citizenship, which exist with deeply embedded dichotomies of rich/poor, white/black, men/women/, abled/disabled, heterosexual/homosexual/LGBTQI and citizen/immigrant/refugee. In this regard, Gutmann (in an interview with Sardoc, 2018: 248) cautions liberal democracies against losing ground in fostering and disseminating mutual respect for different ways of life and different points of view:

> In many places, liberal democracies have retreated from earlier gains they made in toleration, respect, and understanding across divides. We see it in the rise of hate crimes in the United States and throughout much of Europe. We see it in the decreased valuing of freedom of speech. We see it in the way democratic adversaries treat one another as enemies rather than competitors in democratic politics. We see it in bullying in schools and workplaces. We see it in the hardening of far-right and far-left politics, the widening of the gulf in between, and corrosive distrust of information sources and once-respected institutions. At the same time, we have not only witnessed but have been agents pressing hard for more equal freedoms and opportunities for women, people of colour, LGBTQ, and other vulnerable individuals and minority groups. Dire poverty worldwide – a primary barrier to life itself, never mind citizenship education – has also decreased over the past decade.

Therefore, what it means to be a citizen is at once clear and apparent, as it is mired in controversy and upheaval. To Bosniak (2006), although the idea of citizenship is commonly invoked to convey a state of democratic belonging and inclusion, this inclusion is usually premised on a conception of a bounded and exclusive community. In this regard, says Bosniak (2006: 1), '[c]itizenship as an ideal is understood to embody a commitment against subordination, but citizenship can also represent an axis of subordination itself'. On the one hand, as Benhabib (2004: 6) explains, while state sovereignty in economic, military and technological domains has been greatly eroded, it is nonetheless vigorously asserted, and national borders, while more porous, are still there to keep out aliens and intruders. Yet, relegation or exclusion is not limited to those seeking to enter a particular citizenship – as it is with immigrants or refugees. Degrees of citizenship implies that even those who belong politically, legally and civilly might not have access to citizenship's full membership and benefits. Citizens, regardless of nationality, are, of course, hardly homogeneous in terms of their group identities. As entrenched as it is within any community, society and nation-state, diversity presents points of disagreement and conflict, which can play a defining role in the hegemonic structures and discourses of liberal democracies. Individuals and groups who belong to different religions, cultures, ethnicities and tribes, for example, can often not lay claim to equal forms of citizenship.

Every society prescribes its own normativities, which, by default, constructs others' norms, as less than. South African society, for example, continues to propagate an Anglo-Christian normativity. It is important, of course, to be cognizant of the historical onslaughts, which resulted in such a normativity – the successive enslavements of colonialism and then apartheid. Up to 1994, when apartheid ended, the majority of South Africans – those classified as black, Indian and coloured – were not only considered third-rate citizens but systemically oppressed because of their race and ethnicity. Furthermore, although the laws of apartheid have been rendered illegal through the transition to a democracy, the legacies and residues of segregation, discrimination and exclusion continue to live in the corners of public spheres, especially educational institutions. As a result, despite a political climate of a very liberal democracy where equal rights are seemingly afforded equally to all citizens, notions of citizenship, recognition, inclusion and belonging continue to provoke disagreement, conflict and anger, as large sections of South African society continue to live below what is socially humane, and politically viable.

The persistence of an Anglo-Christian normativity has necessarily rendered into subjugation any other norm or way of being. Subjugation and its ensuing tensions take many forms – from language rights, regional autonomy, political representation, education curriculum, land claims to national symbols, immigration and naturalisation (Kymlicka, 1995). South Africa, for instance, has eleven official languages. Although there are attempts at promoting all languages – at least in terms of policy – the attempts have not moved beyond rhetoric, as English remains that language of academic success and economic mobility. In this way, as McKinney (2017: 99) contends, ideological power is exerted through Anglonormativity not only as 'an ethnolinguistic repertoire of whiteness' but as the norm and as synonymous with ideal learners. In the end, says McKinney (2017), it is multilingualism, as opposed to monolingualism, which is constructed as the problem, with the result that those who try to hold onto their indigenous language, or mother tongue, are excluded for failing to assimilate.

Like language, religion and culture hold particular significance for identity formation. Apartheid South Africa provides yet another interesting but disturbing example of assimilation through Christianity – as propagated through a national curriculum, referred to as Christian National Education (CNE). CNE derives from a distinctive interpretation of Calvinism, which suited the Dutch Reformed Church's specific agenda. As a countermeasure to British influence, it propagated an inseparability between the church and the state. For practical purposes, all schooling was to be regarded as church schooling. This meant that regardless of religion, ethnicity or culture all learners in public schools were compelled to learn within a Christian ethos. In this regard, religious instruction were seen as opportunities for evangelism and the nurturing of Calvinist values and principles. It also meant Christian prayers being recited at the commencement and conclusion of the school day, before break-times, before examinations, before sporting events and before school assemblies, which included singing a hymn.

Moreover, particular interpretations of Christianity were used to justify the use of corporal punishment. There was no acknowledgement or inclusion of any other faiths or traditions. Despite immense educational policy reforms post-apartheid, specifically geared at democratic citizenship education and social justice, the dominance of a Christian ethos in most South African schools has seemingly not abated.

STRETCHING THE NOTION OF DEMOCRATIC CITIZENSHIP EDUCATION IN RESPONSE TO ITS PREDICAMENTS

We consider an overwhelming emphasis on a contractual relationship between an individual, others and the nation-state per se as a predicament for the notion of a democratic citizenry. Why? In the first place, when democratic citizenship and education, for that matter, are determined by the idea of a contract between individuals and the state, then immediately the autonomy of the individuals and others in relation with the state seems to become constrained by the very idea of a contract. In such a contractual relationship, an individual cannot autonomously exercise her rights and even responsibilities as she is bound by a contract that involves the state. For example, if the state does not permit the opposition to its rules and regulations by virtue of the contract between state and individual, the latter would be prevented from autonomously exercising its right to dissent. In this way, a contractual relationship seems to undermine an individual's autonomy and the state's responsibility, in turn, to hold an individual accountable to it, perhaps autocratically imposed rule of curbing dissent, such as in the case of several northern African countries. The point we are making is that a contractual relationship between individuals, others and the state does not seem to be plausible to advance the notion of a democratic citizenship. This situation in itself seems to be a dilemma for both the notion of democratic citizenship education.

What exacerbates a contractual understanding of democratic citizenship is, first, that the legitimacy of the contractual relationship constrains an individual's autonomy – that is, an individual cannot autonomously speak her mind. Second, being bound by a contract implies that one's freedom would be curtailed through the relationship that demands that one cannot treat the other with belligerence which often provokes another to think differently. In a nonprovocative relationship, pleasing one another seems to be what drives the relationship. Third, a contractual relationship seems to be prejudiced towards the dominant party, in this instance, the state. If the state decides to undermine the contract, then invariably an individual would be disadvantaged more than the state. Here we specifically think of how an African nation-state prevented oppositional groups from protesting against inhumane policies. Considering that the notion of a contractual relationship through democratic citizenry can become vulnerable to oppression, it seems more feasible to think of democratic citizenship differently. Therefore, we want to propose a different take on democratic citizenship education: a view of democratic citizenship education that transcends the notion of a contractual relationship between an individual, others and the state. It is to such a discussion to which we now turn.

The Ranciérean idea of equality seems to be a more plausible concept according to which one can rethink the idea of a contractual democratic citizenry. Jacques Ranciére (2016: 155) offers an account of human encounters. In this instance, democratic citizenry and education as opens up or disrupts human encounters so that things can be seen anew. For him, it is the idea of disagreement that allows people to reconfigure understandings about human relations. Through disruption, Ranciére (2016: 146) posits humans can reconstruct their encounters in the social world and this implies that they speak as equal beings. Unlike contractual relations, when humans speak as equal beings, they exhibit a capacity to alter encounters. For Ranciére (2016: 155), when individuals exercise their equality, they are no longer dominated and exploited, but they have actually developed the capacity to resist and reject assumptions about themselves and situations – that is, they can and should disagree, which is not necessarily the case as in a contractual relationship.

What follows from the above is that democratic citizenship education in terms of equality seems more feasible than one based on a contractual relationship. When humans engage in encounters, they freely make claims about their lived texts and then make decisions to reconfigure their relationships with others and the state based on agreement and disagreement. In this way, their equal relationships contribute towards their emancipation as they are not coerced by contract to stand by the decisions others made for them. They are engaged in an 'intellectual adventure' (Ranciére, 2016: 139) as they engage in an 'intelligence of anybody' without waiting for confirmation from others. That is, they can express their equal intelligence in a democratic citizenry, and they have the capacity to alter understandings.

In sum, contractual democratic citizenship holds people accountable to one another in terms of legal and judicial policies and procedures, with individuals often succumbing to the authority of a hegemonic state. However, equal democratic citizenship prioritises the autonomy of persons whereby they are summoned to disagree with others in educational encounters. It is the notion of equality that creates opportunities for humans to engage in substantive encounters rather than peripheral ones. When human encounters are inherently substantive, people are bound by their equal intelligences that invariably take issue with notions of race, ethnicity and class because the element of disagreement seems to undermine any superficial and/or peripheral engagement that might evolve. Disagreement is one aspect of human action that does not sit well with contractual relations. Instead, disagreement has the potential to emancipate people from that which might constrain them; that is, their contractual obligation demanded by a thin form of democratic citizenship. A 'thick' notion of democratic citizenship is one guided by equality and the possibility of disagreement. When people of different races, ethnicities and social allegiances engage in encounters, any chance of cultivating equal encounters is premised on the idea that disagreement would challenge them to disrupt forces of domination, narcissism and rebellion, albeit racial bias, ethnic prejudice and social inequality. As argued for elsewhere (Waghid, 2019: 20), humans' 'potential dissensus reached within and about social matters is an affirmation of their equal capacities to reconfigure the world'.

In conclusion, there is much to be said about finding a citizenship of unconditional belonging, but we know, as discussed in this chapter, that there are significant gaps between what is purportedly on offer to citizens, and indeed what is lived and experienced by citizens. Given the embedded hierarchies and truth-claims used to substantiate these hierarchies and hegemonies, it is inevitable that while citizenship locates certain citizens at the centre of its privileges, others are rendered to the margins. The argument that citizenship itself can represent an axis of subordination (Bosniak, 2006) means citizenship is experienced unequally and unequitably. Reasons for unequal or peripheral citizenship vary from identity markers of gender, religion, culture and ethnicity to whether one is an immigrant or refugee. By drawing on Ranciére (2016), we argued that through disruption, humans could reconstruct their encounters in the social world and this implies that they speak as equal beings. As equals, they are no longer dominated and exploited; instead, they have developed the capacity to resist and reject assumptions about themselves and their situations. In this way, their equal relationships contribute to their emancipation as they are not coerced by contract to stand by the decisions others have made for them.

Chapter 3

Race as a Social (Re)Construction of Exclusion

INTRODUCTION

Despite arguments and debates that, conceptually, race is not real, that it is a social construction and reconstruction devoid of any biological and moral significance, race remains a highly visible source of agitation, discrimination and dehumanisation. Arising from this simmering tension is what we understand as relational constructions of 'blackness' and 'whiteness' – which, although framed differently depending on the geopolitical contexts, speak to the same grappling not only on race but on the relational tensions between race as a construct and race as a condition of being human. Of course, such a reification of race in itself poses enormous challenges to the practice of democratic inclusion because claims that race is merely invented would put to rest any argument that race should actually be considered as 'something' that shapes inclusion. Nevertheless, our philosophical take on race itself offers possibilities to rethink democratic inclusion. Likewise, the invisibility ascribed to and owned by 'whiteness' perceivably opens a path of uninterrupted being and thinking. This stands in contradistinction to the lived experiences of 'blackness' where implicit judgements are made before the individual who owns the colour has even spoken.

For democratic citizenship, the dichotomous, at times, oppositional, yet parallel pathways of 'blackness' and 'whiteness' have profound implications. These implications are not limited to states of being; they are on vivid display in who is afforded voice, who is seen, who is recognised and, consequently, who has the power. Similar tensions reside in educational systems and engagements, in terms of who our teachers and academics are and how they present themselves, who our educational leaders are and are presented, what curricula are propagated and, ultimately, what the implications are for democratic citizenship as we continue to sift through prejudicial subthemes of 'white' competence as opposed to 'black' incompetence. As we wade through the thickness of these debates and tensions, we keep our gaze on the implications for education when race is used as a conditional marker of identity not only in the decisions of teaching but in relation to learning. Equally, when race is used to make pronouncements on teaching and learning, the prejudicial implications for such human encounters are even more devastating and indefensible than looking at race through teaching and learning.

RACE AS (MIS)CONSTRUCTED

It is worthwhile at this point to clarify our understanding of race and ethnicity. As South Africans who both lived through the trauma and dehumanisation of apartheid, we are painfully aware not only of the divisions imposed through the rhetoric of race, ethnicity and culture but also that these three categorisations are, at times, used interchangeably, especially in relation to oppression and othering. In turn, how an individual chooses to describe or identify him- or herself can depend on which characteristic holds the greater meaning or depth to that individual. In South Africa, for example, where racial oppression was legitimised and systemised through political structures and governance, citizens might be more inclined to identify themselves in terms of race. This pattern is supported by current institutional practices – public and private, as well as schools and universities – which request and require information based on racial categorisation. This is purportedly done for reasons of transparently managing transformation and democratisation in terms of racial representation. Historically advantaged schools and universities, for instance, are under pressure to show their commitment through racial representation – which, of course, should not be confused with actual transformation processes focussed on creating the spaces necessary for integration, inclusion and belonging.

It is not easy to define race – whether as a sociohistorical process and construct, or as a biological foundation. Appiah (2015: 3), for instance, observes that up to the nineteenth century, race was informed by essentialism – 'The idea that human groups have core properties in common that explains not just their shared superficial appearances but also the deep tendencies of their moral and cultural lives'. People, submits Appiah (2015: 3), thought race was important not just because it allowed one to define human groups scientifically but also because they believed that racial groups shared inherited moral and psychological tendencies that helped explain their different histories and cultures. Often, any account of race seems to be biased towards what is considered as 'white' against what seems other. The point is, construction of race seems to be inherently connected to prejudice towards 'whiteness' as if the latter in itself represents some sort of superiority in relation to an imaginative categorisation of humans.

Perhaps the simplest ideational theory of race, says Appiah (1994: 57), is what we learn when we learn a word like 'race' is a set of rules for applying the term. Everybody who knows what the word 'race' means, he continues, learns the same rules so that while people have different beliefs about races, they share some particular beliefs that define the concept. These beliefs may include the thought that people with very different skin colours are of different races or that one's race is determined by their parents' race (Appiah, 1994: 57). As time progressed, explains Appiah (2015: 4), natural scientists in the 1960s argued that the concept of race had no place in human biology, and social scientists increasingly considered the social groups previously called 'races' to be social constructions. For this reason, social scientists began to use terms, such as 'ethnic' or 'ethnoracial' group, in order to stress the point that they were not aiming to use a biological system of classification (Appiah, 2015).

More recently, according to Appiah (2015: 4), while some philosophers and biologists have sought to reintroduce the concept of race as biological, this argument does not undermine the basic claim that the boundaries of the social groups called 'races' have been drawn based on social, rather than biological, criteria. Regardless, biology does not generate its own political or moral significance. Despite arguments that the concept of race is not real and does not exist, it continues to be construed as an identity marker. Race, says Yancy (Peters, 2019: 663), is a social construction:

> Like marriage, it isn't a natural kind, but a social kind. By this I mean that the concept of race doesn't have a referent in the natural world. There is no *thing* to which the concept of race points. So, it is a concept that is ontologically empty. Yet, it is a concept that exists. Its emergence in the world came from Western Europe. It is a concept that is socially and historically produced and shaped by colonial desire, bad faith, domination, psychological projection, and ontological and epistemic logics that are Manichean in nature.

More troubling, of course, is when essentialist constructions of identity, such as race, are used for segregation, oppression and dehumanisation. Racial realism argues for acknowledging the reality of race as a means to achieve racial justice (Soudien, 2013:16). Racial realists believe that a strategic mechanism for racial justice is to use race as ammunition to fight racism. Despite race being shown as not real, it is viewed as part of one's identity (Soudien, 2012: 19). A politics of recognition, as Ahmed (2004) posits, is also about definition – that is, 'If we recognize something such as racism, then we also offer a definition of that which we recognize'. In this sense, she explains, 'Recognition produces rather than simply finds its object; recognition delineates the boundaries of what it recognises as given'. To Ahmed (2004), it is important to examine how institutions become white by positing some bodies rather than others as the institution's subjects (whom the institution is shaped for, and whom it is shaped by). Racism, she argues, would not be evident in what 'we' fail to do, but what 'we' have already done, whereby the 'we' is an effect of the doing.

Yet, when race is not real, the possibility that it enlarges one's identity can also not be considered real. Consequently, any human experience pertaining to race would invariably be flawed as such an experience in itself would be enframed by a delineation that simply does not exist. One can only conclude that a construction and/or invention of race is meant to introduce a categorisation into human experiences that seem to be meant to undermine such encounters.

At this point of the discussion, it is worth pausing on the South African example, which serves as a discursive context in which race was employed – ideologically, politically, economically and socially – as a brutally dehumanising tool. The fundamental objective of apartheid (literal translation, 'apartness' or separation) was to maintain and ensure 'white' supremacy through the implementation of separation along racially constructed lines, which was formally institutionalised in the apartheid laws of 1948, under the government of the National Party. The Population Registration Act 30 of 1950, as explained by Erasmus (2017: 88–89), legislated the recording of each person's race in South Africa as one of the following: 'white', 'native' and 'coloured', with 'Indian' as a subcategory of 'coloured'. According to Erasmus (2017), under Section 1 of the Registration Act 30 of 1950, the classification of white was defined as 'a person who in appearance obviously is, or who is generally accepted as a white person, but does not include a person who, although in appearance obviously a white person, is generally accepted as a coloured person'. The classification of 'native' referred to a 'person who in fact is or is generally accepted as a member of any aboriginal race or tribe of Africa'. The ruling National Party, which propagated apartheid, says Erasmus (2017), began to use a classification of 'Bantu' instead of 'native'. By 1978, the racial descriptor of 'Bantu' was replaced with the racial classification of 'Black'. In turn, the Population Registration Act categorised 'coloureds' as neither black nor white, positioning 'coloured as an intermediate category between essentialist constructs of "white" and "black"' (Lewis, 1987). To Erasmus (2001: 13), this kind of social engineering encouraged 'coloureds' to believe that they were 'not only not white, but less than white; not only not black but better than black'.

In practice, apartheid ensured stratified citizenship, which not only facilitated physical segregation in terms of residential clustering through the Group Areas Act of 1950 and segregated schooling but literally designed and constructed a society where the different racial groups – classified as 'white', 'black', 'coloured' and 'Indian' – were not allowed to interact. Opportunities in terms of mobility, access, participation and inclusion – whether in education or employment – were directly linked to racial categories. In sum, South Africa's political citizenship project of apartheid was based upon and mobilised through an ideology of 'white' minority privilege at the expense of the exclusion and dehumanisation of all other racial groups. The onset of democracy in 1994 – promulgated through a constitutional democracy – ensures equal rights to all citizens. Despite the huge fanfare that accompanied Nelson Mandela's release – largely described as a pioneer of South Africa's democracy – the ideals of democratic citizenship remain elusive to the majority of historically disenfranchised citizens. The continuing use of racial descriptors has done little to rid South African society of its apartheid-induced intolerance and disregard for difference. Moreover, as is the case in most liberal democracies, just because apartheid or racism is considered as a blight on any society does not mean that racism is eradicated from the spaces and discourses of human engagement and encounters.

'WHITENESS' AS SYMBOL OF RACIAL IDENTITY

Giroux (1997: 376) explains that in the early 1990s, debates on race took a provocative turn as 'whiteness' became increasingly visible as a symbol of racial identity:

> Displaced from its common-sense status as an unnamed, universal moral referent, 'whiteness' as a category of racial identity was appropriated by diverse conservative and right-wing groups, as well as critical scholars, as part of a broader articulation of race and difference, though in different ways and for radically opposed purposes.

Central to theoretical work on 'whiteness' is the attempt to confront 'the issue of white racial identity [and to raise] the questions of when, why and with what results so-called "white people" have come to identify themselves as white' (Roediger, 1994: 75, in Giroux, 1997: 380). Dislodged from a self-legitimating discourse grounded in a set of fixed transcendental racial categories, says Giroux (1997: 380), 'whiteness' is analysed as a lived but rarely recognised component of white racial identity and domination.

'Whiteness', by its very nature, explains George Yancy, is binary and hierarchical. 'Whiteness' is the thesis (that is, it establishes itself as such) and 'racialised' groups that are not white are deemed 'different, deviant, that is, the antithesis' (Peters, 2019: 663–664). As 'a structural, ideological, embodied, epistemological and phenomenological mode of being', 'whiteness', explains Yancy (Blasdel, 2018), 'is predicated upon its distance from and negation of blackness'; neither 'whiteness' nor 'blackness' are based on objective, biological facts, but are 'sites of lived meaning' (Yancy & Del Guadalupe Davidson, 2016: 8). Neither whiteness nor blackness, as racial categories, are objective, biological facts – they are sites of lived meaning (Yancy & Del Guadalupe Davidson, 2016: 8). In Wright's (2015: 2) opinion, determining blackness as a determinable 'thing', as a 'what' or 'who', 'gives us a conceptualisation that exhibits the unnerving qualities as a mirage: from a distance, it appears cogent, but up close, blackness evanesces, revealing no one shared quality that justifies such frequent and assured use of this signifier'.

From Yancy's perspective, the 'terrain of blackness' remains a site of social pathology through the white gaze; the epistemology of whiteness reinforces a black/white binary; it is whiteness that sustains this binary through its transcendental status in relationship to blacks (Yancy & Del Guadalupe Davidson, 2016: 10). To Yancy, 'whiteness'

> is a master of concealment; it is insidiously embedded within responses, reactions, good intentions, postural gestures, denials, and structural and material orders. . . . Whiteness as a form of ambushing is not an anomaly. The operations of whiteness are by no means completely transparent. (2008: 229)

So embedded is the condition of 'whiteness' that it has not been subjected to the same level of scholarly scrutiny and analyses as 'blackness' (Giroux, 1997: 379).

For Yancy (2012: 7), the fact of the matter is that for white people, 'Whiteness is the transcendental norm in terms of which they live their lives as persons, individuals'. The lives of white people are unmarked; they are able to live their identities as unraced, as simply human, as persons. 'Whiteness', says Ahmed (2004), is 'represented as invisible, as the unseen or the unmarked, as a non-colour, the absent presence or hidden referent, against which all other colours are measured as forms of deviance'. It is, of course, only invisible to those who inhabit it. For those who do not, continues Ahmed (2004), it is hard not to see whiteness; it even seems everywhere.

> Seeing whiteness is about living its effects, as effects that allow white bodies to extend into spaces that have already taken their shape, spaces in which black

bodies stand out, stand apart, unless they pass, which means passing through space by passing as white.

People of colour, therefore, as Yancy (2012: 7) explains, 'confront whiteness in their everyday lives, not as an abstract concept, but in the form of embodied whites who engage in racist practices that negatively affect their lives'.

'Whiteness', as Owen (2007: 205) elucidates, operates or functions as a sociohistorical phenomenon that reproduces white supremacy. First, whiteness defines a particular racialised perspective or standpoint that shapes the white subject's understanding of both self and the social world. As a structuring property, states Owen (2007: 206), whiteness situates persons racialised as white in a social location that provides a particular and limited perspective on the world. Second, whiteness defines a specifically racialised social location of structural advantage. Third, the normalisation of whiteness contributes to its transparency. The fourth functional property is implied by the third, explains Owen (2007: 206), namely, that whiteness is largely invisible to whites and yet highly visible to non-whites. Fifth, whiteness is embodied; it is grounded in the interests, needs and values of those racialised as white, so it is founded on the ascribed racial identity of being white (Owen, 2007). Sixth, its borders are continuously being redefined; it is a sociohistorical phenomenon, and theoretical analyses should not reify it as an essential form. And, its seventh functional property is that of violence:

> [n]ot only does whiteness have its origins in the physical and psychic violence of the enslavement, genocide and exploitation of peoples of color around the world, but also it maintains the system of white supremacy in part by means of actual and potential violence. (Owen, 2007: 206)

By identifying and marking 'whiteness', explains Yancy (2012: 7), black people can locate 'whiteness' as a specific historical and ideological configuration; it is in itself an act of situating 'whiteness' within the context of 'material forces and raced interest-laden values that reinforce whiteness as a site of privilege and hegemony'. To many whites, therefore, the process of marking the white body 'is not just difficult, but threatening' (Yancy, 2012: 9). What this process dares to do is not only to mark whites as 'perpetuators and sustainers of racism' but to mark whites as '*raced* beings', as inextricably bound to the historical legacy of the 'workings of race' (Yancy, 2012: 9)

WHITENESS AS ORIENTATED TOWARDS EXCLUSION

Despite the fact that race is not a natural kind, contends Yancy (Peters, 2019: 664), 'it has tremendous social ontological power; the concept is a powerful organizing social vector that functions as if it cuts at the very joints of reality'. The concept of race, he continues, 'constitutes our institutional spaces, our political forms of arrangement, our perceptions, our bodily comportment in space, our organization of lived space and lived experience. In fact, the state itself is a site of racial power'. This power is so embedded that we seldom realise the extent to which the spaces we occupy are orientated around whiteness and exclude non-whiteness. Spaces – the public sphere, schools and universities – acquire the 'skin' of the bodies that inhabit them; 'institutions' as orientation devices take the shape of 'what' resides within them (Ahmed, 2007: 157). When we describe institutions as 'being' white (institutional whiteness), explains Ahmed (2007: 157), 'We are pointing to how institutional spaces are shaped by the proximity of some bodies and not others: white bodies gather and cohere to form the edges of such spaces'. According to Owen (2007: 208), whiteness is a structuring property of modern social systems and, as such, it shapes the formation of both the consciousness of agents in terms of their cognitive and evaluative frameworks and the patterning of social practices. Owen (2007: 208) maintains that if the social world is systematically shaped by the needs, interests and values of whites, then individuals are always already being socialised and acculturated into whiteness, with the consequence that they will internalise cognitive and evaluative schemas that reflect this whiteness. Thus, 'whiteness systematically informs – and deforms – every aspect of the social world' (Owen, 2007: 208).

As black academics in a historically white university in South Africa, for example, we are rendered visible and noticeable in a space, which has yet to reconcile itself with non-whiteness.

In other words, it seems as if our academic work is looked at as being produced by persons who are not white and, therefore, not by an exclusive racial group. Consequently, our contributions to scholarship should be scrutinised more closely concerning whom we are perceived to be. For instance, if a professor's academic work is valued as of high quality, it could erroneously only be so due to such a scholar's whiteness and vice versa. A scholar not considered white is subjected to more scrutiny than would usually be the case.

According to Yancy (2005: 216), the hermeneutics of the body, how it is understood, how it is 'seen', its 'truth' is partly the result of a profound historical, ideological construction. 'The body', he explains, is positioned by historical practices and discourses; 'It is codified as this or that in terms of meanings that are sanctioned, scripted, and constituted through processes of negotiation that are embedded within and serve various ideological interests that are grounded within further power-laden social processes' (Yancy, 2005: 216). When bodies are out of place, says Ahmed (2007: 159), they are out of place – 'Such standing reconfirms the whiteness of the space'. We know that each time we step into the glare of a lecture theatre, certain invisible hegemonies, discourses and worldviews have to be redeciphered to accept that we are indeed present in the space as lecturers. This is not to be confused with an acceptance of any kind. The presumed, yet unacknowledged, privilege of whiteness would first need to be disrupted for this to happen. As South Africans, we continue to make the mistake of ascribing the perceived intrusion of black skins to apartheid. Apartheid, while certainly bolder in its sordid display of racism, is, in fact, whiteness made visible. As Owen (2007: 105) makes us aware, if whiteness is systematically embedded in the social world, 'then local micro-critiques and refusals will be insufficient to disrupt its power to reproduce racial domination'. Instead, he argues, only a theoretical understanding of its central operational properties will provide us with the insight and understanding to devise effective strategies to disrupt and dismantle its hold on modern social systems (Owen, 2007: 105).

What we experience at our university is not inimitable. We have similar experiences at international conferences, when if not who we are, then what we have to say is brought into suspicion. For example, one of us has often tried to include discussions and debates on the African philosophy of education in spaces where Western philosophy remains intact as the only philosophy worth considering. These attempts of considering new forms of knowledge, while listened to, are not engaged with for the purposes of deeper understanding and meaning.

Our experiences have taught us that philosophies of education dare not be associated with what is African because that idea in the first instance essentialises erudition. Such paradoxical views on philosophies of education are forms of essentialising on the grounds that the discourse is conceived only in relation to the perceived whiteness of its scholarship. Hence, it is conceived that Aristotle, Gadamer, Freud, Nietzsche and Habermas were all white males. Their work subsequently elevates philosophy and philosophy of education in the Anglo-Saxon and Continental traditions of thought to the level of a constructed racial hegemony. As it happens, the credible scholarship of Africans through the seminal works of Wiredu, Gyekye and Assie-Lumumba are viewed as secondary to the hegemonic contributions of Anglo-Saxon and Continental thinkers. Not surprisingly, African philosophy of education has always been viewed sceptically at conferences and meetings with an Anglo-Saxon and Continental bias.

However, when the philosophy of education is conceived as a living practice, it might be that the discourse in itself would begin to assume a far more defensible and not 'racial' nomenclature. This is so on the grounds that a living philosophy of education does not focus on who says what and with what specific rationality, but instead on what is more apt for the contextual conditions of our times. In our most recent work, we consider cultivating decoloniality in university education by drawing on a living philosophy of education.

Such a living philosophy of education holds the possibility of rethinking human experience in relation to what it might be and not who advocates what and for whom. Through engaging and sharing real human experiences from and within African societies and universities, we (re)imagine decoloniality as a fiction brought to life through a living philosophy of education. Here, we encourage academics to think of how their research – in relation to teaching, learning and scholarship – can stimulate fictitious imaginaries of a society in which people engage in iterations and the free exchange of provocative ideas without any reference to racial categorisations of being human. We posit that a society might be more imaginative where people live in harmony despite their 'racial' differences that seem irreconcilable. People might even renounce antagonism and encourage the free integration of pluralist ideas of a common humanity (Waghid, Davids, and others, 2020).

The embedded invisibility of whiteness naturally presumes that unless knowledge is Anglo-normative ('around whiteness'), it cannot hold anything worth knowing or learning. The effect of this 'around whiteness', asserts Ahmed (2007: 157), is the institutionalisation of a certain 'likeness', which makes non-white bodies feel uncomfortable, exposed, visible and different when they take up this space:

> The institutionalization of whiteness involves work: the institution comes to have a body as an effect of this work. It is important that we do not reify institutions, by presuming they are simply given and that they decide what we do. Rather, institutions become given, as an effect of the repetition of decisions made over time, which shapes the surface of institutional spaces. Institutions involve the accumulation of past decisions about how to allocate resources, as well as 'who' to recruit. Recruitment functions as a technology for the reproduction of whiteness.

Racial segregation in South Africa spread and thrived in every facet of society – from residences, public spaces and transport to schools and universities. The entire formulation and structuring of higher education for black students by the apartheid state were intentionally set up 'with the responsibility of intellectually and politically winning students to the separate development project [the Bantustan project] and generating the administrative corps for the separate development bureaucracies' (Badat, 1999: 77). The recruitment and appointments of rectors, vice chancellors, academic and senior administrative staff were made by the minister responsible for the various institutions. The logic of the Bantustan project dictated that black educational institutions should be essentially staffed by blacks but that the ideological and political control should be maintained through the employment of predominantly Afrikaner nationalists and white conservatives (Badat, 1999: 71).

Although apartheid as a political ideology has been replaced by democracy, apartheid as whiteness remains intact. As Yancy (2008: 235) observes, '[t]o be white in America [and anywhere else] is to be always already implicated in structures of power'. And although democratic reform has been accompanied by recruitment and employment reform in attempts to redress historical inequities and injustices – otherwise known as affirmative action – the sheer systematicity of whiteness preserves its presence. Whiteness, explains Owen (2007: 209), 'functions in such a way that it maintains the legacy of racial inequality as a central aspect of modern social systems, while at the same time, masking the impact of that history upon the present'. In a South African context, the masking of historical impact takes many forms: from creating impressions of racial transformation through a few strategic and visible appointments to reframing, reinterpreting and justifying racial exclusion through a competence-based language. Framing this multifaceted construction of 'competence' or 'standards', most often, is a 'whiteness', which, on the one hand, 'benefits all whites regardless of their class or gender status' (Leonardo, 2009: 70) and, on the other hand, is used for no other reason but oppression.

One of the biggest challenges to integration in South African schools, for example, resides in the often unchanged composition of teacher demographics, regardless of a dramatic shift in the learner corps. It is fairly common to find diversity limited to learner bodies, with the teaching staff retaining its historical racial identity. The appointment of black teachers at historically white school remains a painfully slow endeavour, with Jansen (2007: 30) asserting that incoming black teachers 'are already framed in ways that disempower them, and the same nurturing and accommodation that is so readily made for novice white teachers seldom apply to novice black teachers'. The struggle to recognise institutional racism, explains Ahmed (2012: 44), can be understood as part of a broader struggle to recognise that all forms of power, inequality and domination are systematic rather than individual. This is not to say that individual racists do not exist – they obviously do – but instead, argues Ahmed (2012: 44), that 'the very identification of racism with individuals becomes a technology for the reproduction of racism *of* institutions'.

Amid the challenges to employing teachers or academics from diverse identities and backgrounds are as many benefits to their inclusion as there are drawbacks to their exclusion. To Ingersoll et al. (2019: 3), demographic parity or inclusion is equally important for minority and majority-group learners; it counters the disparity between the racial and cultural backgrounds of learners and teachers; it provides the context for cultural synchronicity, which allows for minority-group teachers to relate to the life experiences and cultural backgrounds of minority-group learners due to insider knowledge; and can possibly promote culturally responsive teaching (Achinstein et al., 2010).

In sum, democratic inclusion as made manifest in employing teachers from diverse groups allows for the inclusion and articulation of different life-worlds and perspectives, which stands to benefit all learners, teachers and parents, and hence, society. The more learners can engage and learn from those who are different to themselves, the greater and deeper their preparation for engaging with difference, not only at school but later as citizens in a pluralist society. Concomitantly, the less diverse a teacher corps is, the greater the risk of perpetuating existing hegemonies, as defined and trapped in constructions of whiteness and blackness.

Chapter 4

Intersectionality, Race and Ethnicity

INTRODUCTION

Like conceptions of race, 'blackness', 'whiteness', as well as ethnicity and gender, Kimberlé Crenshaw's 'intersectionality' is not without controversy. Emerging from debates centred on critical race theory, Crenshaw (1989) conceives intersectionality as a prism, confirming the multiplicity of identity and its accompanying perceptions and experiences – whereby the intersectional experience outweighs the sum of racism and sexism. Of key interest to Crenshaw, as it is to us, is the need to account for multiple grounds of identity when considering how the social world is constructed. At play here is a theoretical framework through which to consider identity formation and its ensuing multiple points of oppression and discrimination and intersectionality as both methodological and analytical frames and discourses. It becomes necessary that despite the origins of its initial coining, which led to its predominant focus on intersectional minority identities, the concept of intersectionality cannot be limited to the experiences of minority identities or groups (Yuval-Davis, 2011). As we argue, there should be as much attention on the intersectional dimensions that form and sustain privilege and the inclination towards discrimination. To this end, our interest in this chapter is to consider the implications for democratic citizenship education when categories of identities and their accompanying social difference are not used as either privileging or marginalising lenses.

INTERSECTIONALITY: A TANGLED, BUT NECESSARY WEB

The theory of intersectionality emerges from Crenshaw's (1989) argument that when courts treat black women as purely women or purely black, the courts, as they have historically done, have repeatedly ignored specific challenges that face black women as a group. To Crenshaw (1989), courts seem to think that racial discrimination affects all black people across gender and sex discrimination, thereby discounting the specific experiences of women as black or of colour. Yet, contends Crenshaw (1989: 149), black women can experience discrimination in any number of ways and that the contradiction arises from our assumptions that their claims of exclusion must be unidirectional:

> Consider an analogy to traffic in an intersection, coming and going in all four directions. Discrimination, like traffic through an intersection, may flow in one direction, and it may flow in another. If an accident happens in an intersection, it can be caused by cars traveling from any number of directions and, sometimes, from all of them. Similarly, if a Black woman is harmed because she is in the intersection, her injury could result from sex discrimination or race discrimination.

As noted by Haslanger (2014: 216), Crenshaw is not simply concerned with the subjective experience of women of colour and the tools of analysis we use to understand the circumstances they find themselves in. In emphasising the intersectionality of structural oppression, Crenshaw does not argue that we should retreat from analysis but undertake a multidimensional analysis rather than a single-axis analysis (Haslanger, 2014). Following Crenshaw (1989), Bernstein (2020: 321) reminds us that viewing social identities as intersectional has become central to understanding how various dimensions of race, gender, sexual orientation, disability status and class interact to yield more complex forms of discrimination than those suffered by persons who fall under only one category. Sometimes, explains Bernstein (2020: 322), intersectionality refers to members of intersectional social categories, like black women; sometimes it refers to forms of oppression faced by members of such categories; for example, those forms of discrimination faced by black women that are faced neither by women alone nor by black people alone. Sometimes it refers to a type or token of experience faced by members of such categories, as in experiences by black women that are not entirely explicable by appeal to being black or to being a woman; and sometimes it refers to a method of theorising from or about a specific viewpoint, as when one is theorising from the perspective of a disabled Jewish woman. In Bernstein's (2020) opinion, intersectionality is a causal theory, according to which intersecting systems of power produce effects on groups or individuals that would not be produced if the dimensions did not intersect.

The basic idea of intersectionality, says Bernstein (2020: 322), is that forms of oppression stemming from membership in multiple social categories such as 'black' and 'woman' 'intersect and thereby create new forms of oppression that are causally, modally, and relationally different from the constituent forms of oppression merely added together'. Therefore, one finds the combination of 'blackwoman' (Martin, 2000), articulating the connection between race and gender. Similarly, Sherman (2005) has combined the terms 'black' and 'American' – forming blackamerican – to show the connection between race and citizenship. Following suit, Cooke (2008: 91) has constructed the neologism 'Muslimwoman' to illustrate how the veil, real or imagined, functions like race, a marker of essential difference, which Muslim women seemingly cannot escape.

Cooke's (2008) concern was to find a way to draw attention to the post-9/11 collapse of religion and gender into a singular and imposed political category. She wished to highlight the ways in which non-Muslims and Muslim religious extremists alike deploy this newly entwined religious and gendered identification that overlays national, ethnic, cultural, historical and even philosophical diversity in order to control Muslim women. 'Muslimwoman', explains Cooke (2008: 91), draws attention to the emergence of a new, singular religious and gendered identification that overlays national, ethnic, cultural, historical and even philosophical diversity. Underscoring this reconfigured identifications are conceptions and interpretations of cosmopolitanism, which, according to Cooke (2008: 92), are 'at once unifying and diverse because the more people identify with and connect to each other, the more their identities will be hybrid and split among the multiple groups in which they act and want to belong'. As Haslanger (2014: 116) argues, social structures 'intersect and overlap in ways that affect how they oppress/privilege those who are positioned within them':

> [S]exism and racism are two oppressive/privileging structures that have implications for many aspects of one's life, e.g., where one lives, who one lives with, what one does in one's life (employment, education, leisure). One's social circumstances are affected by the combinations of structures one lives in: a White man and a White woman will have different opportunities and will be subjected to different norms because gender structures interact with structures of Whiteness. Similarly, a White woman and a Latina will have different opportunities and face different norms because race structures interact with being gendered a woman.

While social determinables, such as gender, race and class, are inseparable, their social determinates, such as womanhood, blackness and middle-class membership, are not (Bernstein, 2020). To Bernstein (2020), intersectionality is a claim about the inseparability of social determinates, not social determinables. Intersectionality, she continues, is not just about belonging to any gender and any race; it is about belonging to a specific gender (e.g. womanhood) and belonging to a specific race (e.g. being black), and the way those determinate identity constituents interact with each other (Bernstein, 2020: 325).

CONFLATIONS AND CONTROVERSIES

While it might seem that one of the core commonalities between women, race and ethnicity is the embedded controversies within each of its constructions, the reality remains that women are subjected to various levels of marginalisation and oppression on these constructions in the public sphere of citizenship. In this regard, it is especially useful to draw on Crenshaw's (1989: 140) argument that if one is to understand discrimination and subordination practices, then one cannot refer to a single categorical axis. A single categorical axis, contends Crenshaw (1989: 140), 'erases Black women in the conceptualization, identification and remediation of race and sex discrimination by limiting inquiry to the experiences of otherwise-privileged members of the group'. To her, the focus on 'otherwise-privileged group members creates a distorted analysis of racism and sexism because the operative conceptions of race and sex become grounded in experiences that actually represent only a subset of a much more complex phenomenon' (Crenshaw, 1989: 140). To this end, it is Crenshaw's (1989) argument that black women are sometimes excluded from feminist theory and antiracist policy discourse because both are predicated on a discrete set of experiences that often does not accurately reflect the interaction of race and gender. The problems with exclusion, maintains Crenshaw (1989: 140), cannot be solved simply by including black women within an already established analytical structure. This is because the intersectional experience is greater than the sum of racism and sexism; any analysis that does not take intersectionality into account cannot sufficiently address the particular manner in which black women are subordinated (Crenshaw, 1989: 140). Hence her contention:

> Black women can experience discrimination in ways that are both similar to and different from those experienced by white women and Black men. Black women sometimes experience discrimination in ways similar to white women's experiences; sometimes they share very similar experiences with Black men. Yet often they experience double-discrimination – the combined effects of practices which discriminate on the basis of race, and on the basis of sex. And sometimes, they experience discrimination as Black women – not the sum of race and sex discrimination, but as Black women. (Crenshaw, 1989: 149)

To Crenshaw (1989: 154), the value of feminist theory to black women is diminished because it evolves from a white racial context that is seldom acknowledged. As a result, not only are black women overlooked or excluded from the discourse but, argues Crenshaw (1989: 154), their exclusion is reinforced when white women speak for and as them. In this sense, the 'authoritative universal voice – usually white male subjectivity masquerading as non-racial, non-gendered objectivity – is merely transferred to those who, but for gender, share many of the same cultural, economic and social characteristics' (Crenshaw, 1989: 54). In sum, when feminist theory attempts to describe women's experiences by analysing patriarchy, sexuality or separate spheres ideology, it often overlooks the role of race; it neglects the intersectionality of subjugation, marginalisation and oppression (Crenshaw, 1989: 154).

Much of the subsequent discussion of intersectionality in the feminist literature, reports Haslanger (2014), has focussed on the intersectionality of experience. Haslanger (2014: 116) explains that experience is intersectional when it is the result of being socially positioned in multiple categories at once – '[b]ecause I am socially positioned simultaneously as White, able-bodied, affluent, and as a woman, my experience of being a woman is inflected by the ways that these other social positions affect me'. Yuval-Davis (2011: 4), for example, does not limit intersectionality as specific to black and ethnic minority women or marginalised people. To her, intersectionality presents the most valid approach to analysing social stratification as a whole. Intersectional analysis, asserts Yuval-Davis (2011: 4), does not prioritise one facet or category of social difference; instead, it sees difference as mutually constitutive. Bernstein (2020: 323) echoes this assertion that although the literature on intersectionality literature focuses predominantly on intersectional minority identities and unique dimensions of oppression faced by such minorities, it is worth noting that all identities are to some extent intersectional in a broad sense of the term. As such, in the same way that there are distinctive forms of oppression for intersectional minority identities, there are distinctive forms of privilege for nonminority ones (Bernstein, 2020). A white upper-class man, for example, explains Bernstein (2020: 323), is privileged in ways not entirely reducible to the joint features of being white, being a man and being upper class.

To return to Crenshaw's (1989) argument, however, it would be shortsighted to think that all women – regardless of race and ethnicity – experience the public sphere in a similar fashion. In the same vein, it would be contentious to assume that the experiences of black males are the same as that of black females. With black women as the starting point, maintains Crenshaw (1989: 140), 'it becomes more apparent how dominant conceptions of discrimination condition us to think about subordination as disadvantage occurring along a single categorical axis'. Moreover, 'this single-axis framework erases Black women in the conceptualization, identification and remediation of race and sex discrimination by limiting inquiry to the experiences of otherwise-privileged members of the group' (Crenshaw, 1989: 140).

In turn, the greater or the more visible a female's affiliation to a particular identity marker, the greater the risk of differential treatment and discrimination. Consider the specific example of Muslim women who opt to wear the hijab in liberal democracies. Some liberal democracies in Europe have embarked on questionable actions on what they describe as regulating the dress code of Muslim women. These actions are justified because, first, it is presumed that Muslim women do not wear the hijab voluntarily; they are forced to do so by their husbands or other male relatives. Second, arguments advanced by liberal democracies view the hijab as a symbol of backwardness and oppression, and as such, it is irreconcilable with the principles of liberal democracy. As such, the hijab is used and misconstrued as a literal veil, which purportedly prevents Muslim women from actively participating in the public sphere (Petzen, 2012). And third, because Muslim women are presumably being forced to wear the hijab, they are being oppressed and are, hence, in need of emancipation by liberal democracies.

The interest and implications of this debate are twofold. On the one hand is the singular axis through which Muslim women are conceived and categorised as a homogeneous group of oppressed women who have no autonomy. On the other hand is the witnessing of hegemonies, which dictate the look and form of what constitutes 'acceptable' citizenship, or what is commonly referred to as 'our way of life' (Khiabany & Williamson, 2008: 71). Of obvious and deeper concern is when these same hegemonic discourses depict hijab-wearing Muslim women as a threat to security – that is, when they are constructed 'as a visible sign of distrusted difference, dangerous, and resistant through a strong discourse of security' (Golnaraghi & Dye, 2016: 145). From what is already a prevailing pattern of interference and intrusion on the part of liberal democracies, since the problem with the hijab lies with liberal democracies, the narrative being constructed places the source of the tension with Muslim women. It is not that liberal democracies have a problem with hijab-wearing Muslim women; it is that Muslim women are failing or refusing to assimilate into that which constitutes the citizenship of liberal democracies – by refusing to remove their hijabs.

The objectification of women's bodies is, of course, not a new phenomenon. The scholarly interest in Muslim women, in particular, explains Kirmani (2009: 49), has its foundations in the Orientalist fascination with the veil and the harem, which helped to construct a picture of Muslim women as symbols of the brutishness of colonised peoples and the symbolic 'other' to Europe's rational civilisation. What is new, however, is the positioning of veiled Muslim as sites of conflict. In referencing *l'affaire la voile* (the veil affair) in France, Benhabib (2011: 168) contends that women's bodies have become 'the site of symbolic confrontations between a reessentialized understanding of religious and cultural differences and the forces of state power, whether in their civic-republican, liberal-democratic or multicultural form'. To her, the nature of the tension between religion as a political theology and the forces of state power can, at best, be described as a clash between identities of a collective nature (as envisaged by the nation-state) and identities of an individual nature (as manifested in different religions and cultures). As a result of this tension and within the crossfires of debates and clashes, Muslim women are becoming increasingly stigmatised, criminalised and marked for social and economic exclusion (Petzen, 2012: 97). Accompanying this stigmatisation is a deep sense of alienation, leaving Muslim women torn between entering the public square on stipulated conditions or retreating to the private sphere, where they can be who they are.

UNDOING INTERSECTIONAL POLEMIC OF RACE AND ETHNICITY

If definitions of race – regardless of their unfoundedness – have primarily been couched in biology, then ethnicity has equally problematically been associated with culture. As Zack (2017: 93) observes, ideas of race sometimes overlap with ideas of ethnicity. She explains as follows:

> Hispanic/Latinx Americans believe that despite their official classification as an ethnicity, they are treated as members of a nonwhite race. Also, historically in the United States, immigrants who were first identified as members of nonwhite races, such as Italian, Irish, Polish, and Jewish people became re-identified as racially white, over several generations of assimilation. There are other complexities: Jews are now considered primarily a religious group, although it is assumed they also have a distinct ethnicity. (Zack, 2017: 93)

Ethnicity as related to race, continues Zack (2017: 93), becomes even more complex if we compare ideas of human difference globally, such as socioeconomic and mixed-race notions of race in Brazil and the caste system in India. For reasons such as these, Appiah (1994: 117) contends that racial and ethnic identities are 'essentially contrastive and relate centrally to social and political power; in this way they are like genders and sexualities'.

On the one hand, explains Gracia (2007: 1), is the factual challenge, which argues that 'the concepts of race and ethnicity do not correspond to anything real outside the mind and therefore need to be abandoned'. As is the case with women and race, references to ethnic labels often assume that ethnic groups are homogeneous. On the other hand, says Gracia (2007: 3), is the epistemic challenge, which argues 'that we have no effective criteria to establish membership to races or ethne'. Appiah (1994: 118) explains that ethnic identities are created in family and community life. These, along with mass-mediated culture, the school and the college, are, for most people, the central sites of the social transmission of culture (Appiah, 1994). According to Appiah (1994: 118), distinct practices, ideas, norms go with each ethnicity in part because people want to be ethnically distinct: because many people want the sense of solidarity that comes from being unlike others. With ethnicity in modern society, he continues, it is often the distinct identity that comes first and the cultural distinction that is created and maintained because of it, not the other way around (Appiah, 1994: 118).

In response to attempting to address the epistemic challenge as encountered in the concept of ethnicity, states Gracia (2007: 4), philosophers have sought to develop alternative ways of thinking about race and ethnicity. One group proposes to replace race with ethnicity; another replaces race with racial identity; and yet another alternative combines race and identity either in the concept of ethnic race or in the concept of racial ethnicity; and another, race and ethnicity, but develops new ways of conceiving them (Gracia, 2007: 4).

Notwithstanding the aforementioned polemic about 'race', we concur with Zeus Leonardo (2009: 69) that 'race' is, in fact, a creation or invention of European humanism designed to limit theories of the human to those with white skin in particular, and those broadly conceived as white by the master race. Leonardo (2009: 69) adds that 'race' is a social construction invented by whites. In his words, 'race is understood as a differential system of advantage that benefits all whites regardless of their class or gender status'. In other words, 'race' seems to be used by whites to exploit, denigrate and exclaim their superiority over people of colour. Consequently, race abolitionists, like ourselves, appeal to humans to disengage from using 'race' as 'race' and, by implication, whiteness 'has never existed for other reasons besides oppression ... [thus] proclaiming it as utterly negative ... a form of violence that seduces ... white ... to a privileged place in race' (Leonardo, 2009: 70).

The point is that whites are not born (in the biological sense) but made within a social, racial formation system. In this regard, Leonardo (2009: 71) posits, 'Whiteness is the oldest child of race, which is the empty and therefore terrifying attempt to build an identity based on what one isn't and on whom one can hold back ... [being] nothing but oppressive'. What follows is that if racial demystification were to occur, and we would argue in the latter's defence, a process of 'unthinking whiteness' among those who see themselves as white ought to take place. Here, Leonardo (2009: 71) is quite explicit when he avers 'race relations begin to unravel since white exists with its Other and both are burst asunder in the process'.

What follows from the aforementioned explication of 'race' is that constructing 'race' and whiteness is an illusion or ideological chimaera summed up by Miles (2000: 135) as follows:

There are no 'races' and therefore no 'race relations'. There is only a belief that there are such things, a belief which is used by some social groups to construct an Other (and therefore the Self) in thought as a prelude to exclusion and domination, and by other social groups to define self (and so to construct an Other) as a means of resisting that exclusion, Hence, if it is used at all, the idea of 'race' should be used only to refer descriptively to such uses of the idea of race.

Although Miles's pronouncement on 'race' has its merit, it remains somewhat problematic for the reason that those who are urged to renounce white and whiteness in the first place believe themselves to be white people. As Leonardo (2009: 73) puts it, whites 'have built a society after their own image'. That is, although 'race' is socially constructed and not real in the biological sense, it exists and is sustained in real terms. In other words, that 'race' should not exist is different from saying that they currently do not exist (Leonardo, 2009: 73).

Revisiting the issue of racism, we can sum up a few categorisations: first, to be racist is to dislike or hate black persons and other minorities (Trepagnier, 2006: 3). For instance, regarding everyday racism, black women report that those identified as whites often seem surprised to find a black person has a professional qualification – that is, blacks are actually educated or successful (Trepagnier, 2006: 3). Second, racism is also institutional or systemic that includes racist practices of individuals, the economic and political power of whites over blacks, racial economic inequality, and racist ideologies, attitudes and institutions created to preserve white privilege and power (Trepagnier, 2006: 4). Third, silent racism is of two types: stereotypical images based on misinformation about blacks prevalent in culture; and paternalistic assumptions based on a sense of superiority found in some relations among blacks and whites (Trepagnier, 2006: 6). Again Trepagnier (2006: 3) avers that

> silent racism is not the same as prejudice, generally perceived as bigoted attitudes toward minorities. Instead, she contends, silent racism is closely linked to images, attitudes, and fictions that link and buttress systemic racism that constitutes a broad white-racist worldview. (Trepagnier, 2006: 6)

Following the discussion thus far, it would seem that the most likely way through which to address the polemics, as constructed and presented by race and ethnicity is, as Valdez and Golash-Boza (2017: 2256) suggest, to engage in dialogue – 'not because ethnicity and race are the same thing, but because they are distinct concepts that bring different relationships and perspectives to bear on pressing social issues'. Valdez and Golash-Boza's (2017) point echoes that of Yuval-Davis (2006: 201) when she posits that ethnic and racial divisions relate to 'discourses of collectivities constructed around exclusionary/inclusionary boundaries' that can be constructed as 'permeable and mutable to different extents and that divide people into "us" and "them"'. To Yuval-Davis (2006: 201), such boundaries 'are often organized around myths (whether historically valid or not) of common origin and/or common destiny'. To truly understand how ethnicity and race operate as distinct yet intersecting dimensions of identity and collectivity, explain Valdez and Golash-Boza (2017: 2258), the process of racialisation must be situated within dynamic or contingent group-specific contexts that racialise ethnic groups in particular ways. This includes recognizing that intersections of ethnicity and race occur within a racialised social structure – one which is embedded in a system of white supremacy.

To Valdez and Golash-Boza (2017), although ethnicity and race are both socially constructed, they are not socially constructed in the same ways. Instead, race and ethnicity explain different aspects of inequality conditioned by distinct social relationships embedded within a highly stratified context. According to Valdez and Golash-Boza (2017: 2257), race and ethnicity reflect fundamentally different inter/intragroup relationships and dynamics that contribute to the life chances of group members. In this regard, they cite the example of structural racism, which has been identified as a critical factor in explaining health disparities between black and white Americans, but this relationship is less examined or understood for Asian and Latinos in the United States.

So, the question arises, how do the views of racism guide an understanding of democratic citizenship education? In the first place, the possibility that humans, especially minorities and black persons, would live out their democratic agency and citizenship would be heavily curtailed because hatred towards the other would undeniably prevent people from engaging with one another about matters that concern them. Second, if racist attitudes and the exercise of political and economic power over minorities and blacks were to prevail, the latter's sense of belonging in a democratic society would be undoubtedly curtailed. Third, if silent racism enhanced through bigoted attitudes were to dominate human relations, it seems very unlikely that the cultivation of a socially just community would ever be realised. In short, democratic citizenship in the realm of any form of racism, as espoused earlier, would be quite impossible to pursue. We argue that democratic citizenship education in the realm of prevalent racism – everyday, systemic or silent – and a racial-ethnic ideology that subverts human living would be impossible to flourish. Any form of racism is pernicious, and people should take a stand against it.

Chapter 5

Gender and Citizenship

INTRODUCTION

In the liberal tradition, citizens are presumed to have equal status, rights and responsibilities. Yet, regardless of presumptions of equality, which extend into access and participation in the public sphere, citizenship is not without constraints and prejudices – as confirmed by a communitarian interpretation of citizenship. The modern state and its public sphere have long been infused with barricaded constructions of masculinity, which have remained intent upon delineating itself not only from femininity and its accompanying language but any claims to emotion. Women, therefore, have long been relegated to the outside of circles and substructures of society. And, despite the purported commitment by liberal democracies to gender equality, the meaning and scope of what it means to engage on an equal basis as a woman continues to be wrapped in dispute. In this chapter, we draw on a number of theorists', such as Butler (1995), Appiah (2015), as well as Young's (1989), depiction of oppositional citizenship – that is, one which makes a separation between the universality of the public realm of citizenship and the particularity of private interest. We are especially interested in the dichotomous constructions of masculine-reason as opposed to feminine-emotion, and how this opposition or tension serves to support and foment discursively disparate forms of citizenship for women.

WOMEN AS GENDER

Butler (1995: 6) argues that if gender is the cultural meaning that the sexed body assumes, then a gender cannot be said to follow from a sex in any one way. Taken to its logical limit, says Butler (1995: 6), 'The sex/gender distinction suggests a radical discontinuity between sexed bodies and culturally constructed genders'. The presumption of a binary gender system, she continues, 'implicitly retains the belief in a mimetic relation of gender to sex whereby gender mirrors sex or is otherwise restricted by it' (Butler, 1995: 6). Moreover,

> When the constructed status of gender is theorized as radically independent of sex, gender itself becomes a free-floating artifice, with the consequence that man and masculine might just as easily signify a female body as a male one, and woman and feminine a male body as easily as a female one. (Butler, 1995: 6)

On the one hand, states Butler (1995: 4), the masculine/feminine binary constitutes an exclusive framework in which specificity can be recognised. In other words, a male is a male because he is not a female. On the other hand, says Butler (1995: 4), the specificity of what constitutes the feminine is fully decontextualised and cut off analytically and politically from class, race, ethnicity and other axes of power relations that not only constitute identity but renders the idea of a singular notion of identity as a misnomer. In Butler's words (1995: 7):

> It would make no sense, then, to define gender as the cultural interpretation of sex, if sex itself is a gendered category. Gender ought not to be conceived merely as the cultural inscription of meaning on a pregiven sex (a juridical conception); gender must also designate the very apparatus of production whereby the sexes themselves are established. As a result, gender is not to culture as sex is to nature; gender is also the discursive/cultural means by which 'sexed nature' or 'a natural sex' is produced and established as 'prediscursive', prior to culture, a politically neutral surface on which culture acts.

Gender, therefore, following Butler (1995), is fluid, and the construction of women is contextualised and linked to categories which themselves are in flux. Hence, Riley's (1987: 35) description of women as a 'volatile collectivity' in which female persons can be so differently positioned that the apparent continuity of the subject of 'women' cannot be relied upon. In recognising the limitation of the 'woman', Butler (1999: 5) contends, first, that gender is not always composed coherently or consistently in different historical contexts. Second, gender intersects with social, class, ethnic, sexual and regional modalities of discursively comprised identities.

To Butler (1995: 5), the political assumption that there must be a collective or universal basis for feminism is often conflated with a similar assumption that women's oppression is singular in nature. Implicit in this assumption of the singularity of experience is the belief that women own a singular identity regardless of culture, religion, class or race, which, of course, as we will show throughout this book, is not the case. Moreover, as Pateman (1989: 2) observes, to discuss 'women's issues' is not the same as engaging with or contributing to feminist theory. The distinctiveness of feminist theory, she continues, is that 'it insists that a repressed problem lies at the heart of modern political theory – the problem of patriarchal power or the government of women by men' (Pateman, 1989: 2). We concur with Pateman (1989: 4) that although women have not entirely been excluded from participation in the institutions of the public world, they have, however, been incorporated into public life in a manner different to that of men. The challenge, therefore, as addressed through third-wave feminism, is to develop a feminist theory and politics that honour contradictory experiences and deconstruct categorical thinking; that challenge notions of universal womanhood; and that present ways in which groups of women confront complex intersections of gender, sexuality, race, class and as age-related concerns (Krolokke & Sorenson 2006: 16–17).

Following this discussion and in setting the tone and grounds for the ensuing discussions in this book, we are drawn to MacKinnon's (1983: 635) emphatic argument:

> Feminism has no theory of the state. It has a theory of power: sexuality gendered as gender is sexualized. Male and female are created through the erotization of dominance and submission. The man/woman difference and the dominance/submission dynamic define each other. This is the social meaning of sex and the distinctively feminist account of gender inequality.

What feminism does is to bring into contestation the predominance of male perspectives and the systemic hegemonies, which sustain these perspectives. The subjugated status of women is necessary for the perpetuation of these hegemonies. The male perspective, asserts MacKinnon (1983: 636), 'enforces woman's definition, encircles her body, circumlocutes her speech, and describes life'. In other words, for as long as all individuals accept these hegemonies, the predominance of the male worldview cannot be disrupted. For as long as women in the circles of men's perspectives, they will continue to live by their norms and binaries, which necessitates women's less-than construction. Feminism, says MacKinnon (1983: 637), criticises this male totality and insists on the realisation of 'a more whole truth'. A 'more whole truth' considers that which is beyond and outside of a male perspective; it recognises other ways of being and thinking, and it affirms rationality as much as emotion. To MacKinnon (1983: 637), the idea that feminism 'affirms women's point of view by revealing, criticizing, and explaining its impossibility' is not a dialectical paradox. Instead, to her, feminism is 'a methodological expression of women's situation, in which the struggle for consciousness is a struggle for a world: for a sexuality, a history, a culture, a community, a form of power, an experience of the sacred' (MacKinnon, 1983: 637).

GENDERED CITIZENSHIP

Issues of women and citizenship, states Friedman (2005: 4), are not merely about the deprivation of political rights of women. What needs to be taken into account, she elaborates, is the gendered nature of the practices, assumptions and contexts of political citizenship itself. To Munday (2009: 252), 'The most important assumptions are that definitions of citizenship rely on the public/private dichotomy and that the citizen is conceived of as an abstract, disembodied individual'. In both liberal rights and civic republican traditions, continues Munday (2009: 252), the concept of citizenship rests on the distinction between the public and private spheres, with citizenship being firmly located within the realm of the public. The public citizen is seen to be 'a rational, unemotional individual able to transcend their own body, interests and partiality' and are free to perform their public role as citizens (Munday, 2009: 252). Habermas (1974: 49) has long conceived of the public sphere 'as a realm of our social life in which something approaching public opinion can be formed'. In mainstream political theory, says Pateman (1989: 4), the public sphere is assumed to be capable of being understood on its own, 'as if it existed *sui generis*, independently of private sexual relations and domestic life. The structure of relations between the sexes is ignored, and sexual relations stand as the paradigm of all that is private or non-political'.

Nevertheless, asserts Pateman (1989: 4), the meanings of 'private' and 'public' are mutually interdependent; the public cannot be comprehended in isolation. As Yuval-Davis (1997: 21) explains, citizenship rights are anchored in both the social and the political domains; without 'enabling' social conditions, political rights are vacuous. To Friedman (2005: 4), the public and political spheres in which citizenship is paradigmatically conceptualised and practised are spheres based predominantly on modes of living and attributes that are stereotypically male. Men, argues Pateman (1989: 4), are presumed to possess the capacities for citizenship; they are presumed to be able 'to use their reason to sublimate their passions, develop a sense of justice and so uphold the universal, civil law'. By contrast, women, womanhood and women's bodies represent the private; they represent all that is excluded from the public sphere; they cannot transcend their bodily natures and sexual passions; women, presumably, cannot develop the same political morality as men (Pateman, 1989: 4).

Joseph (1996: 6) explains that women have been crucial in establishing and maintaining nations' boundaries and are often made into their symbolic markers. This is evident by the institutions and processes nations subsidise to control women's reproduction, maternal rights, productivity and wealth. Laws regulating marriage, naturalisation, inheritance and property are among the formal means nations use to define and defend the boundaries of their communities (Joseph, 1996). History reveals that courts and policy-makers repeatedly told proponents of women's rights that not all citizens were created equal – 'that women's unique physical characteristics and social role justified differential treatment in a wide range of areas despite their claims to equal citizenship' (Grossman & McClain, 2009: 9). Marriage, for example, has long had profound effects on the citizenship and civil rights of women concerning property ownership and contract (Grossman & McClain, 2009). In a number of Middle Eastern countries, the imposition of 'male guardianship' – whereby women cannot be unaccompanied by a male relative in the public sphere – is just one manifestation of the peripheral citizenship enforced through gendered binaries. Women continue to inherit less than their male relatives; they are deemed as having less status as legal witnesses than men, and they often have no legal rights to initiate divorce or maintain custody of their children (Joseph, 1996).

Issues of gender and citizenship, according to Joseph (1996: 6), are not limited to legal issues but also raise issues of practice, specifically the practices that comprise governance. What the law affords in principle and what women experience in practice is often quite different. According to Joseph (1996: 6), making sense, therefore, of the role of the state in mediating citizenship rights requires seeing the multiple and conflicting interests represented and embodied in the state, as well as recognising the often contradictory practices carried out by the various agencies and agents of the state in relationship to women. That the practices of citizenship, following Friedman (2005), are largely based on modes of living, that even when the rights and privileges of political citizenship are made available to women, practical as well as conceptual obstacles may make it difficult for women to avail themselves fully of these options. Even as an increasing number of women enter the world of work and occupy positions traditionally reserved for males, they continue to carry the significant burden of domestic duties and child care (Munday, 2009).

Indeed, it is because of this unequal burden of responsibility that men are able to take on any additional political roles and activism, as demanded by the public sphere. Women, maintains Joseph (1996: 7), are recognised and addressed as citizens in the context of their positions within patriarchal structures, as subordinate mothers, wives, children or siblings. And, as their relationship to the state is often mediated through family ties, women are often conflated with children as mutually dependent upon men – 'or the extent that women are recognised as valued members of society, their value is often abstracted and depicted in terms of their familial roles and sacrifices, notably as mothers' (Joseph, 1996: 7). Given the importance of family in patriarchal structures, argues Joseph (1996: 7), women are expected to continue to prioritise their subordinate familial roles even when they achieve public status as individuals, including, in some cases, powerful public positions. Certainly, states Okin (1989: 4), 'the fact that women are doing more paid work does not imply that they are more equal'. Instead, what is typically the case, the more productive she is in the world of work, the more she needs to prove herself worthy of that position. In turn, she might face increasing criticism of her perceived neglect of her family – constituted as her primary responsibility. Consider, for example, women leadership in educational settings, such as schools and universities. What becomes apparent immediately is that in most settings, women in leadership positions are underrepresented. Even where a school has a much higher number of females than male teachers, the principal, in all likelihood, will be male. The underrepresentation of women in leadership positions is exacerbated by findings that women leave management in the same numbers that they enter (Moorosi 2010). External and internal pressures brought about by the construction of women as the primary caregiver hold serious consequences for both men and women in that it perpetuates existing hegemonies of power and discourses. For this reason, Okin (1989: 4) maintains that until there is justice within the family, women will not be able to gain equality in politics, at work or in any other sphere.

WOMEN, CITIZENSHIP AND INVISIBILITY

Generally, universalist conceptions of citizenship presume that the status of citizenship transcends difference and particularity. In other words, different categorisations of group identities – whether race, religion, class, culture, ethnicity or gender – have no impact on the rights afforded through being a citizen. With equality conceived as sameness, posits Young (1989: 250), the ideal of universal citizenship carries at least two meanings in addition to the extension of citizenship to everyone. First, 'universality defined as general in opposition to particular; what citizens have in common as opposed to how they differ'; and second, 'universality in the sense of laws and rules that say the same for all and apply to all in the same way; laws and rules that are blind to individual and group differences' (Young, 1989: 250).

However, as we have already begun to show in this chapter, and as Young's (1989: 251) argument shows,

> [T]he ideal that the activities of citizenship express or create a general will that transcends the particular differences of group affiliation, situation, and interest has in practice excluded groups judged not capable of adopting that general

point of view; the idea of citizenship as expressing a general will has tended to enforce a homogeneity of citizens. To the degree that contemporary proponents of revitalized citizenship retain that idea of a general will and common life, they implicitly support the same exclusions and homogeneity. . . . Second, where differences in capacities, culture, values, and behavioral styles exist among groups, but some of these groups are privileged, strict adherence to a principle of equal treatment tends to perpetuate oppression or disadvantage.

Following this, Young (1989: 253) hones in on women's particular experiences, contending that the discourse that links the civic public with the fraternity is not merely metaphorical. The idea of the modern nation-state, says Young (1989: 253), has been established by men. Moreover, while the modern state and its public realm of citizenship have been paraded as constitutive of universal values and norms, these norms, maintain Young (1989: 253), have been derived from specifically masculine experiences. Yuval-Davis (1991: 59) advances a similar argument in her description of a community, assumed to have a 'natural' and 'organic wholeness'. These include 'militarist norms of honour and homoerotic camaraderie; respectful competition and bargaining among independent agents; discourse framed in unemotional tones of dispassionate reason'. By so doing, she continues, 'modern men expressed a flight from sexual difference, from having to recognize another kind of existence that they could not entirely understand, and from the embodiment, dependency on nature, and morality that women represent' (Young, 1989: 253). As a result, argues Young (1989: 253), 'the opposition between the universality of the public realm of citizenship and the particularity of private interest became conflated with oppositions between reason and passion, masculine and feminine'. This, states Young (1989: 253–254), is evident and instituted in a moral division of labour between reason and sentiment; with identifying masculinity with reason; and femininity with sentiment, desire and the needs of the body. Moreover, emotions, sentiment and bodily needs are relegated and confined to the private sphere of the home and family – 'The generality of the public thus depends on excluding women, who are responsible for tending to that private realm, and who lack the dispassionate rationality and independence required of good citizens' (Young, 1989: 254). This community, asserts Yuval-Davis (1991: 59), assumes a given collectivity; the community does not conceive of itself 'as an ideological and material construction, whose boundaries, structures and norms are a result of constant processes of struggles and negotiations or more general social developments'. Any dynamic notion of 'citizenship' must start from the processes which construct the collectivity and not just assume it.

While it is indeed true that women, today, have more opportunities in the public sphere, than they have previously experienced in terms of access and participation, their presence remains a contested one. Fine (2002: 26), for example, describes the particular experiences of women as 'the presence of an absence'. That is, that while women are present in terms of educational achievements, the workplace, the political and public sphere, generally, their presence neither confirms a 'presence' nor equality in terms of citizenship. There are particular challenges that are unique to women's experiences – directly or indirectly. For instance, particular positions' occupation does not necessarily imply the same degree of empowerment and being seen as that afforded to males in the same position. In higher education workspaces, for example, explains Jackson (2019: 696), female academics are more likely to be recognised by supervisors for achievements that are service-oriented, such as administrative work and teaching, rather than research, in environments where research is clearly more prized. In addition, women are often expected to do equal research to men while taking on more service and teaching. In sum, asserts Jackson (2019: 697), women are not treated the same as men in higher education, by students or colleagues. They are expected to take on more caring, interpersonal roles and succeed in them by being nice, supportive and not too bossy.

Women, submits Yuval-Davis (1991: 9), have paradoxical relationships to collectivities of belonging – ethnic, national, religious. Although men and women are identified as members of the collectivity in the same way that men are – as in a university faculty – there are expectations and nonexpectations specific to women. Consider, for example, who dominates departmental, committee or faculty meetings. Consider who takes the longest turns to speak and who speaks over and interrupts women as they speak. While men lay claim to particular 'truths' and uncompromised 'ways of being', which stem from sociohistorical norms and traditions, women are expected to succumb or face being challenged and possibly, marginalised and excluded. There are power dynamics at play that render female academics' thinking and contributions less-than-significant and less-worthy to take into consideration. Belonging is determined by the extent to which women are prepared to turn a blind eye, to oblige the dominant discourse and ethos. Any resistance by women is perceived negatively and as nonconformist, placing at risk the sense of belonging afforded to women by men. The significance of the latter sentence is not limited to the precariousness of belonging, but rather that the degree of belonging is not determined by the extent to which female academics might find points of resonance and familiarity in a department or faculty, but by whether or not her male peers grant her acceptance. To this end, it is necessary to pay attention to the very concept of belonging, which, of course, might or might not occur across horizontal and vertical lines of existence.

Female academics, for example, might find that their belonging resides in the extent to which they are prepared to 'disappear' from the scene – that is, the extent to which they are prepared not to be seen and heard – bringing us back to Fine's (2002) 'presence of an absence'. Others might find that their belonging depends on the extent to which they are prepared to participate in the dominant, masculine ethos and banter. In either case, the sense of belonging of female academics, at times, depends on whether or not they are prepared or not to assert their own voice. In other words, silence is not to be confused with no sound or nonarticulation; silence is either deafening when women *choose* not to speak or not to act. Based on research in her own higher education work environment, Ahmed (2015) reports that the situation wherein some men sexually touch or dismissively speak to some women is often not seen as a problem for everyone because to recognise it would be to label normal acts of some or a few men as deviant. As Ahmed (2015) explains, to label these acts as deviant or predatory would amount to identifying something bad about the status quo – 'killing joy' (Ahmed, 2015). That female academics might feel disempowered to challenge this behaviour says as much about the predicament of females in the workplace as it does about females in the public sphere.

DISRUPTING DISCURSIVELY DISPARATE FORMS OF CITIZENSHIP FOR WOMEN

Before we analyse and disrupt forms of citizenship for the subject of women, we first look at the masculine/feminine binary in which the specificity of women can be recognised. It seems to us as if talking about a masculine/feminine binary involves separating and identifying men and women. So, like men, women are identified in terms of biological, linguistic and cultural differences, but more poignantly in relation to their political intersections (Butler, 2007: 19). Following Judith Butler (2007: 22), we would argue that it seems more apt to describe women in relation to their political acts, rather than according to 'a normative telos of definitional disclosure' or some dualist structure oppositional to men. Women as a subject of feminism are most appropriately analysed in terms of their convergences within the social field of race, class, and ethnicity and their political oppressions subjugated by human relations of domination and exclusion (Butler, 2007: 6).

The question remains, how do disparate forms of citizenship respond to the aforementioned claims of being women? First, women should be constructed as beings with political agency – that is, those who have the capacity for reflexive mediation (Butler, 2007: 195). In other words, women can reflect substantively on who they are in relation to others. Women see themselves as coexistential with others and that they can shape political practices with intractable depth and substantiveness (Butler, 2007: 200).

Second, as autonomous beings, women can critique deconstruction through which they can redescribe possibilities of sexuality and gender that already exist (Butler, 2007; 203). For instance, following Butler (2007: 2001), women can 'disrupt the foundations that cover over alternative cultural configurations of gender'. Now when a new form of disruptive politics vis-a-vis women are in becoming, citizenship can no longer remain confined to an existing politics of belonging and responsibilities, but rather to rethink existing configurations of citizenship in relation to a more liberatory form of feminist politics.

Considering that citizenship education, first, involves the cultivation of democratic rights (Pashby, 2008: 19), a reconfigured politics of feminism holds that the recognition of women's bodily integrity and the development of effective legal sanctions against rape, violence and enforced sex in domestic life should be practised in line with a renewed feminist critique (Benhabib & Cornell, 1994: 11). In other words, citizenship education has to be changed in line with the demands of women's democratic rights against the extreme violation of such rights. Second, citizenship education is evoked as a site for social justice in which humans enact their responsibilities (Pashby, 2008: 18). A reconfigured notion of feminism denies being dictated certain roles: being someone's daughter, someone's wife and someone's mother (Benhabib & Cornell, 1994: 12). Instead, feminists begin with the encumbered self (situated self) but view the renegotiation of women's psychosexual identities and their autonomous reconstitution by individuals as essential to women's human liberation (Benhabib & Cornell, 1994: 13). In this regard, Benhabib and Cornell (1994: 14) draw on Simone de Beauvoir's epitaph: 'One is not born but becomes woman' to make the argument that gender is not just a fact of embodiment; instead, it is a project of genderisation that takes place within a field of social relations that constrain the freedom of the subject woman from the start. Thus when women exercise their human responsibilities in society – that is, their citizenship responsibilities, they do so without being blind to the gender subtext of their societies (Benhabib & Cornell, 1994: 11).

Third, citizenship education emphasises women's sense of belonging. The latter implies that women's bodies should be treated as encumbered selves, that is, as feminist subjects that turn out to be discursively constituted by the very political system supposed to facilitate their emancipation (Butler, 2007: 3). Put differently, avers Butler (2007: 3),

> [i]t is not enough to inquire into how women might become more fully represented in language and politics . . . [f]eminist critique ought also to understand how the category of 'women' . . . is produced and restrained by the very structures of power through which emancipation [and by implication women's belonging] is sought [and secured].

In sum, the presumption of a binary gender system not only retains existing hegemonies by restricting the thinking and practices of one gender (female) in relation to another but indeed provides the foundational framework for public and private objectification and oppression of women. Instead, what needs to be taken into account is how conceptions of citizenship rely on the public/private divide and how this divide entrenches division between male-rationality and inclusion and belonging, and female-emotion and exclusion and non-belonging. Finally, women's democratic rights, social responsibilities, inclusion and sense of belonging can most appropriately be procured when new possibilities for women's political agency emerge in the realm of citizenship education.

Chapter 6

Equality as an Imperative for Democratic Citizenship Education

INTRODUCTION

Notions of equality – whether legal, political or moral – have always been at the core of democratic politics. Equality maintains the equilibrium of citizenry – that is, that all human beings enjoy the same levels of equality. To Rancière (2002), for example, equality is not a quality of society. Instead, it is a fundamental and inalienable quality of persons and interpersonal relations. As such, he believes that equality is not a goal but a presupposition. Inasmuch as democracy, in turn, presupposes that all its citizens are equal and should be privy to the same set of rights, inequality is an inevitable part of society. On the one hand, society produces and reproduces inequality through its hierarchical structures and hegemonies. In South Africa, notions of inequality were embedded in a dyadic relationship of white superiority and black inferiority. Whites are superior because blacks are inferior; concomitantly, blacks are inferior because of whites' superior stature. Similar constructions exist concerning gender, religions, sexuality and, of course, class.

On the other hand, inequality reproduces itself. Those who are on the receiving end of unequal practices and treatment experience great difficulty disrupting preconstructed norms. It serves the privilege of hegemonies to maintain inequality. Therefore, it follows why Rancière (2002) conceives equality as a quality of the individual rather than society. As such, the individual has the political agency and autonomy to counter inequality (without having to wait on society) and lay claim to equality when this right is being deprived.

Now, although there are multiple notions of equality espoused in liberal democratic theory, we are interested in a notion of equality that can enhance democratic citizenship education. For this reason, we are attracted to Rancière's idea of equality which he couches as equality for recognition (Rancière, 2017: 87). It is such an idea that we examine and explore in relation to democratic citizenship education.

ON PRESUPPOSING EQUALITY

Equality, says Rancière (1999: 19), is an 'empty freedom' that everyone possesses. As such, there is nothing within the concept of equality that differentiates between people. In other words, explains May (2009: 6), 'Politics cannot rely on an essence, whether it be blackness, the feminine, an indigenous character, etc., out of which it emerges'. In this sense, politics (the state) cannot protect the particular qualities or the expression of particular essences (May, 2009). To Rancière (1999), equality is the equality of anyone and everyone. This does not mean that the empty freedom of which he speaks is without content. The equality that is presupposed in political action is a certain equality of intelligence, which recognises that all human beings can think and, hence, act. To Rancière (1991: 46), 'it's enough for us that the opinion be possible'. The idea that all people have 'equality of intelligence' serves as the foundation to Rancière's (1991) argument that equality should indeed be the assumption from which all people should operate. It is true, explains Rancière (1991: 73), 'that we don't know that [wo]men are equal. We are saying that they might be. This is our opinion, and we are trying, along with those who think as we do, to verify it. But we know that this is the very thing that makes a society of humans possible'.

Rancière's (2002: 223) uncompromising insistence that '[e]quality is a presupposition, an initial axiom – or it is nothing' confirms that human beings should not wait to be treated as equals by others. Instead, human beings should simply and decisively presuppose and claim equality as their own and then act upon it – that is, act as they are equal to all others. To wait for equality to be given to one, or to pose equality as a goal, contends Rancière's (2002: 223), is to surrender it to the 'pedagogues of progress, who widen endlessly the distance they promise they will abolish'. In insisting that an individual has a capacity to presuppose his or her equality, Rancière (1999: ix) recognises, on the one hand, the inherent inequalities embedded within society. '[P]olitics [. . .] is that activity which turns on equality as its principle', and, on the other hand, an individual's capacity to change and disrupt those inequalities. All people, contends Rancière, have a capacity to think, speak and act freely to take a stand; they might not all have the same opportunities and abilities, but they do have a capacity – described by him as 'equality of intelligence' (1991: xxii). Instead of equality emerging from a political process, explains May (2009: 5), it must be conceived as the presupposition of those who act – '[i]t must be the expression of political actors rather than the possession of a political hierarchy'. The fundamental assertion, states Ruitenberg (2015: 5), is:

> By speaking to you, I assume we are equals, me capable of saying something intelligible, you capable of understanding what I say. Or vice versa: By listening to you, I assume we are equals, you capable of saying something intelligible, me capable of understanding what you say. As soon as the people speaking and listening do so within a social order, the inequality of their places and ranks in that order – whether of kinship, of class, of gender or any other system of places and ranks – begins to chafe against this fundamental equality.

Traditionally, says May (2009: 4), there is general agreement that equality is, first and foremost, a matter of what people deserve – it is a matter of what they should receive – referred to as distributive theories. Distributive theories, explains May (2009: 4), address what kinds of distributions ought to be made of the social goods. To May (2009), however, to think about equality in terms of distribution is problematic and should therefore be rejected. First, a distributive theory implies that a distributor (often, the state) is responsible for ensuring both the distribution and the maintenance of the proper distribution. Second, it implies a passivity on the part of those who receive the distribution. 'The people living in a particular society do not, unless they form part of the distributing class, have anything to do with equality other than to be the object of it' (May, 2009: 4–5). Implicit in a distribution theory, therefore, is a presumption of not only inequality but an incapacity by an individual to act on that inequality. To May (2009: 5), its sustains 'a hierarchical view of society in which the members of that society are conceived as individuals pursuing disparate and unrelated ends that the state helps them more or less to achieve' – hence Rancière's emphasis on the individual, rather than society. If it were up to the society, women would continue to be subjected to a different set of codes of conduct and norms when it comes to accessing the world of work or the public sphere. If it were up to the society, women would continue to be measured in terms of their roles as wives, mothers and caregivers and nurturers instead of coupling these qualities with others equally honourable, which extends beyond domesticity. These norms and tropes are only brought into disrepute when individuals express their contestation and begin to resist. People, regardless of hierarchical ranks assigned through societal structures, are able to recognise their own discrimination or marginalisation and have the capacity to speak out.

In breaking with traditional conceptions of democratic citizenship education, Rancière's (1991) argument starts from a premise that all people are already intelligent – they are 'speaking beings' (1991: 11). To Rancière (1991: xxii), 'An equality of intelligence rather than an inequality of knowledge, posits equality, just as the act of explication posits inequality'. This is not to say that all people need to be equally capable of the same intelligence levels; 'an equality of intelligence' implies a capacity to think in relation to the public sphere. Unless people are deeply damaged in some way, argues May (2009: 7), they are 'capable of creating meaningful lives with one another, talking with one another, understanding one another, and reasoning about ourselves and our [their] situations'. Although difficult and complex, at times, social and political contexts, continues May (2009: 7), 'do not involve essential mysteries that we are in principle incapable of comprehending without the assistance of a savant of some sort. In short, we are capable of formulating and carrying out our lives with one another'. Taking equality as presupposition, therefore, explains Ruitenberg (2015: 2),

> means we do not ask how we may help people achieve the equality of consciousness that would allow them to reflect on their situation intelligently; rather, we ask what new possibilities emerge when people are treated as if they already have equality of consciousness and already reflect intelligently upon their situation.

ON EQUALITY, RECOGNITION AND DEMOCRATIC CITIZENSHIP EDUCATION

Previously we have argued for a notion of democratic citizenship education grounded in claims of deliberation, belonging and recognition (Waghid & Davids, 2018). For humans to deliberate implies that they articulate their truth claims, and simultaneously, others listen with an intent to talk back. Deliberations do not just require articulations and listening but some critical engagement with the thoughts of others that are responded to for the sake of either improving or refuting the judgements deliberated upon. Equally, when humans stake their claims to belonging, they announce themselves as being present without a hindrance of exclusion by others. Thus, at the core of cultivating a democratic citizenry, people are urged to recognise one another in an atmosphere of mutuality, agreement and dissensus – meaning that people do not always concur on all matters. And, considering that democratic citizenship education is being expanded, it makes sense to assert that people's deliberations, sense of belonging and recognition for that matter are guided according to the educational encounters upon which they embark.

Now, unlike our previous work that merely connected the idea of democratic citizenship education to the notion of recognition, specifically that of equality, we now offer an expanded version of this relationship based on the seminal thoughts of Rancière (2017). So, the question is, what more does equality offer democratic citizenship education? Of course, when we recognise other persons, there is an obligation on our part that we treat them as equals (Rancière, 2017: 84). This means that we not only recognise their abilities to speak their minds and to shape arguments but also that they can be held accountable for their own acts – that is, their judgements and responsibilities. In this regard, Rancière (2017: 87) posits that 'an active [democratic] citizen [is] a person who was able to speak for him- or herself, an independent person, which means an owner, somebody who doesn't depend on another person for his [or her] living'. In our previous elucidation of such a Rancièrean position, we focussed quite narrowly on just the autonomy of an individual concerning speaking her mind. As stated previously, 'When a person is considered equal to another person, she is able to speak her mind. That is, she can articulate herself and in the process give an account of her understanding of this or that situation' (Waghid & Davids, 2018: 8). However, now we want to extend such a claim of equality concerning an independent person who does not depend on another for her living. If one is not dependent on another person for one's living, one is capable of generating work for others – that is, as Rancière puts, he or she is an 'owner'.

To be an owner of property, a car or a cat is not entirely different from being the owner of one's living. One does not own an animal because one can exploit the animal for some reason or another, for instance, exhibiting the animal in some show that accrues a monetary gain. However, when the animal takes ill, one is expected to take it for attendance to a veterinary hospital. Owning a cat, therefore, comes with responsibility. In this sense, ownership of something or someone does not just confirm one's possessions, but rather the responsibility is in ensuring that what one claims to own is cared for. In terms of equality, to be an 'owner' of something or someone implies that one does not just speak independently, but one also assumes responsibility for one's speech so that responsible actions can ensue and be sustained. And, to act responsibly, one is or should be in a position to respond to a situation and concomitantly to be capable of doing so. If one cannot assist one's animal during its illness and respond to its discomfort in some way, one would not be acting responsibly. Responsibility depends on both capability and response. If one can pursue the latter – capability and responsiveness – one can be said to be an owner that acts with responsibility or equality for that matter.

The question is, what does one do when one speaks with equality? First, one speaks autonomously and, in turn, demands that someone else listens to one. In other words, the practice of equality is concerned both with the speaker and listener. When democratic citizens speak equally, they are concerned with their speech and how others interpret or reinterpret their speech. In this way, deliberative encounters underscored by equality are concerned about both speakers and listeners' presence. That is, no one dominates deliberative encounters, but rather the act of recognition in the sense that someone has something worthwhile to say that someone else finds worthwhile listening to. This is what we understand Rancière (2017) has in mind when he posits that active citizens are, in fact, speakers and listeners. In addition, democratic citizens are not just speakers and listeners but also responsible beings because they assume responsibility for their speech acts.

One of the reasons post-colonial (and post-apartheid, in the case of South Africa) societies find it so difficult to shift beyond a politics of hatred and mistrust is that political leaders do not responsibly take ownership of their speeches. Simply put, they simply do not act recognisably responsible. Evidence of the latter can be found in the ongoing feuds between Northern Sudan and Southern Sudan, a situation that undermines the politics of democratic citizenship education. Here, as in South Africa, speech is uttered with scant regard for any harmful effects. Claims to freedom of speech are often abused in the spewing of vitriol, which highlights not only an undermining of democratic encounters but creates unequal spaces between those who occupy positions of power and those who do not. This is especially worrying when it becomes apparent that, on the one hand, the very inequality that characterised apartheid, and which led to the pursuit of democracy, is now reperpetuated in harmful and irresponsible speech and action. On the other hand, there are similar concerns that the very kinds of presuppositions to equality and activism concerning protesting against an apartheid ideology are now misconstrued as out of place in a democracy. Stated differently, the democratic government incorrectly believes that because the twin-goal of eradicating apartheid and the onset of democracy has been achieved, they (the government) are beyond reproach. The government wrongfully believes that the demise of apartheid has somehow dispelled all forms of inequality, when, in fact, the reality is that apartheid or racial inequality not only persists in individual speech and action but that other tropes of inequality, such as gender or class, are an inevitable part of any society.

IMPLICATIONS FOR TEACHING AND LEARNING

The argument that schools, as social institutions, are by definition places and spaces of the perpetuation of inequalities and social hegemonies are fairly common. Schools, according to Masschelein and Simons (2013: 16), are criticised for abusing their power, openly and clandestinely, in order to further other interests; for facilitating subtle mechanisms that reproduce social inequality, despite the scholastic narrative of equal opportunities for all. Furthermore, there is neither equal access nor equal treatment, and even if there were, discrimination continues to exist in the larger society and the labour market (Masschelein & Simons, 2013: 16). Since the implementation of desegregation, schools in South Africa have witnessed significant migration patterns – as parents and learners attempt to access historically advantaged schools, which not only are better resourced in terms of infrastructure and facilities but, generally, have lower learner-to-teacher ratios. The historical privilege of these schools has allowed them to maintain their privilege through exorbitant fees, which attracts a certain kind of learner and parent and keeps the majority of parents and learners at bay. By contrast, historically disadvantaged schools, characterised by, and because of their dismal infrastructure and inadequate facilities – no sporting facilities, no library, no science laboratories – are unable to charge the kinds of fees, which would allow them to employ additional teachers to alleviate the burden of high learner-to-teacher ratios, or to improve their facilities. As a result, the kinds of inequalities enforced during apartheid have not been undone through the legal or constitutional end of apartheid.

Moreover, despite the remarkable work, talent and commitment from teachers and principals in deeply impoverished areas and school communities who try their best to provide quality education and who often achieve much more than teachers in privileged and well-resourced schools, learners in South African schools are not privy to equal education and equal opportunities. Inequality continues through residual legacies and through configurations of new forms of inequality, which made manifest predominantly through socioeconomic disparities. Despite expansive political, social and economic reform, race continues to matter. When one considers exit-level grade 12 results, which, in turn, determine access to higher education or other types of higher education, 'white' learners continue to outperform their peers, which, of course, continues a discourse of inequality along racial binaries. Hence, the accusation that what makes the school perverse is that it stubbornly continues to believe in its autonomy, freedom and neutral pedagogical power of judgement, which supposedly serves to guarantee equal opportunities or justify unequal treatment (Masschelein & Simons, 2013: 16).

For the school and the teacher, the learner's equality is a practical hypothesis – it is not a scientific certainty – which one strives to verify as one teaches (Masschelein & Simons, 2013). It is to be expected, contend Masschelein and Simons (2013: 62), in carrying out this verification, the teacher can and will take the individual learner, his or her situation and questions into consideration. 'But this attention to differences belongs to the realm of teaching itself and is separate from the construction of an education system based on so-called factual or natural differences and inequalities'.

There are, of course, problems with an argument that presupposes that inequalities might also not arise from the realm of teaching itself. It is also not an uncontested given that all schools and all teachers presume all learners possess an 'equality of intelligence' (Rancière, 1991: xxii). Despite the immense ethical implications at play here, the reality is that for some teachers, judgements about a learner's capability or intelligence are not based on what emerges from the teaching and learning encounter but rather are based on race indicators, gender or ethnicity. Recently, a white teacher at a private school in South Africa was found guilty and subsequently fired on a charge of racism. According to newspaper reports, the teacher told 'black' learners that they were only getting good marks because they sat next to 'white' learners. He is alleged to have told a 'black' learner after a test, 'You disappointed the blacks by getting a good mark'. He also allegedly told a 'black' scholarship learner who got a good mark, 'Well done, you've started thinking like a white boy' (Anderson 2017). Evident from this disgraceful encounter is the uncomfortable reality and realisation that learners and learning are not necessarily immune to teachers' biases and prejudices. Indeed, these biases have the power to render certain learners inferior, less intelligent and unequal to others – misrecognising not only the capabilities of learners but also who they are and what they have the potential to become. Teachers, by virtue of their position and pedagogical authority, are able to either instil hope or inflict harm; they are able to either perceive and engage with learners as equally intelligent and with equal potential, or they can allow their own misguided notions of inequality in terms of race, gender, class, ethnicity, culture, sexuality, to determine how they engage with learners, and as such, impede the potential of learners and their learning. What makes any form of inequality especially problematic is that its affliction is not limited to what happens within a classroom or school; inequality has deep-seated consequences for other forms of social, personal and economic inequality.

Despite these criticisms and lived experiences of inequalities within and produced by schools, these criticisms do not account for the full picture of schools, and hence, teaching and learning. To Masschelein and Simons (2013: 60), the claim that the school reproduces social inequalities perverts and misunderstands the concept of the school as such. On the contrary, they argue, more than anything else, schools are adept at creating equality. To them, '[i]t is exactly in (re)cognising this that the dream of social mobility, social progress and emancipation – which, in all cultures and contexts, has been rooted in the school since its invention – is nourished' (Masschelein & Simons, 2013: 60). Similarly, as Ruitenberg (2015: 5) asserts, insofar as citizenship education is concerned with equality, the school may not be the best or primary location for such education. In other words, schools and education offer the best chance for learners to shift out of past inequalities and inequities. To Masschelein and Simons (2013: 61), the elements that 'make' the school – suspension, profanation, the world, attention, discipline, technique – are connected, and can be connected to the experience of ability and possibility. In other words, scholastic space arises as the space par excellence in which equality for all is verified. Thus, this equality becomes the starting point, an assumption that time and again is verified (Masschelein & Simons, 2013). The equality of each student, states Masschelein and Simons (2013: 60), is not a scientific position or a proven fact but a practical starting point that holds that 'everyone is capable'. In this regard, continue Masschelein and Simons (2013: 60), there are no grounds or reasons to deprive someone of the experience of ability – that is, the experience of 'being able to'.

Schools and teachers, explain Masschelein and Simons (2013: 62), who depart from a premise that all learners have equal ability, place everyone in an equal initial situation and provide everyone with the chance to begin – something, they maintain, can become a 'public good'. Here, it is necessary to again revisit Rancière's (1991) *The Ignorant Schoolmaster*, in which he recounts the experiences and learning of the teacher, Joseph Jacotot. The French-speaking Jacotot was to teach some Flemish students. While he could speak only French, his students could only speak Flemish (Dutch). To assist him with this language dilemma, Jacotot suggested that his students read François Fénelon's novel, *Télémaque* – that they should 'learn the French text with the help of the translation' (1991: 2). Prior to the encounter with these students, Jacotot believed that good teaching required explication – 'according to an ordered progression, from the most simple to the most complex' (199: 3). But he had not offered any explanations to the Flemish students:

> He had not explained spelling or conjugations to them. They had looked for the French words that corresponded to words they knew and the reasons for their grammatical endings by themselves. They had learned to put them together to make, in turn, French sentences by themselves: sentences whose spelling and grammar became more and more exact as they progressed through the book; but, above all sentences of writers and not of schoolchildren.

Jacotot, explains Rancière (1991: 3), had realised 'the logic of the explicative system had to be overturned' (1991: 6). Explication, states Rancière (1991: 6), 'is not necessary to remedy an incapacity to understand'; 'To explain something to someone is first of all to show him he cannot understand it by himself'. And by so doing, one (the teacher) assumes superiority over others (learners). This assumption does not speak to a preexisting inequality but rather to an inequality that is initiated and cultivated by the teacher. Based on what he experienced with his students, Jacotot proposes a 'universal teaching', which, according to Rancière (1991: 16), 'has existed since the beginning of the world, alongside all the explicative methods . . . there is no one on earth who hasn't learned something by himself and without a master explicator'. Neither Jacotot nor Rancière (1991), therefore, is proposing the demise of the teacher. As Ruitenberg (2008: 3) explains, there is still a place for teachers in universal teaching, 'but the difference between teachers and students is one only of *will*, not of *intelligence*'.

The teacher who uses the method of universal teaching, continues Ruitenberg (2008: 3), assumes that the student is capable of learning and understanding. Universal teaching encourages the student to use the same intelligence he or she has used for learning many other things without explication – by paying close attention, comparing and verifying. To Ruitenberg (2008: 4), universal teaching illustrates that 'the assumption of inequality underpinning explicative pedagogy is not simply the representation of the fact of inequality, but rather a generative hypothesis of inequality that can be replaced by the hypothesis of equality'. Put differently, it is possible to teach as if all learners or students are equal. But, following Ruitenberg (2008) and Rancière (1991), teaching as if people are equal can only reside within teaching, and hence, the teacher. Teaching as if people are equal cannot become the guiding principle of schools or school systems because schools are state institutions predicated upon ideas of social order (Ruitenberg, 2008). So, too, argues Ruitenberg (2008: 5), 'democracy cannot be a principle guiding schooling for the same reason that universal teaching cannot be a principle guiding schooling: Both universal teaching and democracy are expressions of equality, while schooling is not'. According to Ruitenberg (2008), the best that schools can do is to create spaces and opportunities so that universal teaching can occur. This means recognising the capacity of both teachers and learners or students as having 'equality of intelligence', with an equal will to come to speech, exercise their autonomy and take responsibility for such actions.

In this chapter, we paid particular attention to recognising an individual's (a teacher's) capacity to act responsibly and presume an equal capacity for learning without explications from a teacher. Drawing on the story of Jacotot, as recounted in Rancière's (1991), *The Ignorant Schoolmaster*, we showed that an explicative system that relies on hierarchical constructions between teachers and learners, and implies a teacher's superiority over a learner's inferiority, has to be replaced with a universal form of teaching. The central point highlighted here is that when a teacher presumes him or herself to be the only authority in the classroom, he or she relegates learners to a status of unequal inferiority. This inequality did not exist before learners entered the encounter with the teacher. It is the teacher who has the capacity to recognise an 'equality of intelligence', and it is the teacher who can choose to engage with learners as equals, thereby evoking their will to learn. Hence, while it might not be possible for schools to depart from a guiding principle of universal teaching – since schools are not spaces of equality – it is indeed possible for teachers and learners (as individuals) to recognise equality within each other – regardless of social rank, gender, race, ethnicity, culture or sexuality.

Chapter 7

Underrepresentation as a Pervasive Impediment to Democratic Education

INTRODUCTION

Depending on the context, the terms 'representivity' and 'representation' are used interchangeably – both lending themselves towards informing and shaping deliberative democracy. In turn, representation or representivity is not without criticism, as inevitable questions arise regarding substantive or meaningful, as opposed to symbolic or quota representivity. Generally, debates on matters of representivity – in terms of gender, race and ethnicity – are a common centrepiece of liberal democracies. In South Africa, debates on representation are intertwined, at times, subsumed, in agonisms and antagonisms of transformation – locating representivity as a desired antithesis of underrepresentivity. If one considers Hanna Pitkin's (1967) ideas on representation, it becomes apparent that perhaps the binary construction between representation and underrepresentation might not be as clear and self-explanatory as one might think. On the one hand, necessary questions arise regarding the substantiveness of representation, specifically, as to whether it dispels underrepresentation. On the other hand, what are the risks of attempting to address underrepresentation through representation if what is achieved is framed only in terms of symbolism?

REPRESENTATION AS PRESENCE

While there is disagreement about what is understood by the term 'representation', Pitkin (1967: 8) asserts that it does have an 'identifiable meaning, applied in different but controlled and discoverable ways in different contexts'. She defines representation or 're-presentation' as 'a making present again' (Pitkin, 1967: 8). Taken generally, Pitkin (1967: 8–9) continues, representation 'means that making present *in some sense* of something nevertheless not present literally, or in fact'. Forty years later, after first writing about representation, she concedes that the concept of representation is puzzling not because it lacks a central definition 'but because that definition implies a paradox (being present and yet not present) and is too general to help reconcile the word's many senses with their sometimes conflicting implications' (Pitkin, 2004: 335). At the centre of the puzzle, it would seem, is the very relationship between democracy and representation. The concept of democracy, explains Pitkin (2004: 337), originated with the ancient Greeks, with Athenian democracy being won 'by political struggle, from below, and it was direct and participatory to an astonishing degree', and unrelated to any notion of universal human rights. The Greeks thought of other peoples (barbarians) and women as 'generically incapable of politics'; their democracy had nothing to do with representation (Pitkin, 2004: 337).

By contrast, states Pitkin (2004: 337), representation as a political idea and practice emerged only in the early modern period and had nothing to do with democracy. Representation emerged as a matter of royal convenience and administrative control. It became institutionalised through repeated practice and slowly came to be considered a matter of right rather than a burden, although even then, the selection of delegates was by no means democratic (Pitkin, 2004: 337). In this sense, to Pitkin (1967, 2004), one must know the context in which the concept of representation is placed to determine its meaning. To this end, she identifies at least four different views of representation: formalistic representation, descriptive representation, symbolic representation and substantive representation. To her, each of these views provides a different approach for examining representation, which, in turn, can also provide different standards for assessing representatives (Pitkin, 1967). Formalistic representation refers to the institutional arrangements that precede and initiate representation; it has two dimensions: authorisation and accountability; descriptive representation refers to the extent to which a representative resembles those being represented; symbolic representation refers to the ways that a representative 'stands for' the represented; and substantive representation, which she describes as the most crucial dimension since it involves 'acting in the interest of the represented, in a manner responsive to them' – that is, acting in the interest of those being represented (Pitkin, 1967: 209).

Following Pitkin (1967), explains Celis (2013: 180), research strands within the broad field of political representation have focussed on 'the congruence between the input (citizen's interests) and the output of political decision – and policy-making as a way to measure the quality of substantive representation'. This focus on congruence, says Celis (2013: 180), assumes that citizens' interests are stable and exist prior to and apart from politics and representation. It conceives of interests as 'available' to representatives that the legitimacy or representativeness of laws and policies can be determined by comparing them to public opinion. Pitkin's (1967) view of substantive representation, for instance, observes Celis (2013: 180), has been criticised for no longer applying to contemporary political reality – 'where meaningful social and political collectivities are evaporating, and representative democracies face high levels of party dealignment and electoral volatility, rendering citizen's interests and needs difficult to decipher for representatives'.

Conceiving of representation as a 'construction', asserts Celis (2013: 180), inevitably disconnects, to a certain extent, representation from 'the people'. The question that arises is whether all claims by representatives constitute substantive representation or whether a representative's actions or claims need to fulfil certain criteria to qualify as 'good' substantive representation. An immediate example, which comes to mind is that of School Governing Bodies (SGBs) in South African schools. The South African Schools Act No. 84 (DoE 1996a) proposes a partnership between the state, parents, educators and learners concerning the funding, governance and organisation of schools. The primary motivation for governance reforms in post-apartheid South Africa is the democratisation of schooling. The *Education White Paper 2* (DoE 1996b: 16) states that 'governance policy for public schools is based on the core values of democracy', including representation of all stakeholder groups, participation, tolerance, rational discussion and collective decision-making. The assumption is that through decentralising and devolving authority and responsibility, the onus of governance is transferred from the principal to parents (Bush & Gamage, 2001). To this end, all public schools are required to elect a representative body, comprising the principal, educators, support or administrative staff, and parents, who constitute the majority group, and who occupy all office-bearer positions – specifically, that the number of parents in any SGB must be at least half plus one of the total combined number of members with voting rights. The rationale for this power balance, explains Karlsson (2002: 329), is that parents of enrolled learners have the greatest stake in the school's development and the quality of teaching and learning within the school.

Philosophically, SGBs are considered an enactment of the principles of inclusivity (of all stakeholders) and decentralisation (of authority) and have been constructed to address a very specific agenda, namely, cultivating democracy through parental and community participation. Politically, however, SGBs have brought to the fore unabridged disparities between historically advantaged and historically disadvantaged schools and communities

– bringing into question not only its philosophical imperative but its impact upon the fostering of a democratic society. The SA Schools Act (DoE 1996a) extends substantive decision-making authority to SGBs. These include adopting a constitution, determining policies for admission, language, religion, homework, discipline, extra-mural programmes, maintaining school property, recommending the appointment of staff and managing the finances, which includes setting school fees (DoE, 1996). On the one hand, these responsibilities require a sophisticated level of skills and knowledge, which, given the hugely disparate socioeconomic gaps between schools in South Africa, the majority of SGBs might not be capable of assuming. On the other hand, even if parents have the social and intellectual capital to fulfil the mandate of governance, the parents elected onto SGBs might, in fact, not be representative of the parent body of the school.

The Ministerial Review Committee on School Governance (DoE, 2004: 52) found that even in racially homogenous settings, the better educated and the economically more stable members of the community dominate the SGB. Even where learner demographics have shifted, and the school is quite diverse, parent representation on the SGB remains in the control of the (historical) dominant racial group (Karlsson, 2002; Van Wyk, 2007). Van Wyk (2007: 132) reports that principals justify parents' unequal representation on SGBs with statements like 'black parents did not want to become involved' – even when this perception has never been verified. In this regard, Karlsson (2002: 331) maintains that while SGBs have been introduced to democratise schools, the South Schools Act (DoE, 1996a) 'provides no mechanism for avoiding and overcoming a reenactment of the traditional power relations in South Africa in terms of gender, class and race. Nor does it ensure racial heterogeneity when constituencies comprise diverse racial groups'.

Following this, recent normative theories on representation, says Celis (2013: 180), attach great importance to responsiveness and reflexivity as indicators of the quality of representative democracy. According to her, reflexivity 'is a system-capacity criterion that focuses on the extent to which representation furthers contestation and objection from the represented to determine legitimacy' (Celis, 2013: 180). Legitimate representation, Celis continues (2013: 180), is here conceived of as a 'mobilisation democracy' that enables the interaction between claims and contesting counterclaims and empowers the represented to form their own preferences and to make their own judgements. It would seem, therefore, if we return to the example of SGBs that representation or representivity does not release all other stakeholders (in this case, parents) from their responsibility of mobilising democracy such that what unfolds is legitimate – both in terms of representation, and what is being propagated.

REPRESENTATION AS AN ACT OF EDUCATION

Representation for analytic philosophers has mostly been associated with knowledge claims outside of the mind. Such philosophers, like Richard Rorty (1979: 3), have been centrally concerned with the task of a theory of knowledge that they considered as a representation of reality (Rorty, 1979: 3). Thus for Rorty (1979: 9), a theory of representation depends on the assumption that there are enduring constraints on what can count as knowledge. Representation implies that there is a reality in terms of which knowledge can and should be externalised. As aptly stated by him, '[w]e must get the visual, and in particular the mirroring, metaphors out of our speech altogether' (Rorty, 1979, 379). Following Rorty (1979: 372), the analytic philosophers' task becomes one of edifying philosophy in the sense of what they represent is focussed on continuing a conversation rather than discovering the truth. Put differently, representation of knowledge is a form of inquiry through which ideas are made known to the self and others. The idea of representation as an inquiry about knowledge and representation in terms of presence, might at first glance, seem paradoxical. However, when one relooks, making knowledge claims known as inquirers are first and foremost concerned with the reality and, therefore, the presence of the inquirer. In this sense, one could argue that Pitkin's (1967) idea of representation constitutes a neo-Rortyan notion of presentation. And an idea of representation this chapter seemingly builds. Simply put, making representation known again is connected to an idea of externalising claims about knowledge in which an inquirer holds a centralist position – that is, a position of presence.

What follows from the aforementioned elucidation of representation is that any absence of or lack of representation is a notion that does not hold conceptually on the grounds that inadequate representation misrecognises presence. In other words, if humans, say minorities, are not represented, then educationally speaking, they are absent from or invisible to the encounter. Consequently, the idea of underrepresentation suggests that some people are absent from the encounter and, hence, the encounter can no longer be one – at least not an educational one. For this reason, we claim that under-representivity is a pervasive impediment to educational encounters. The question is, what does an absence of or a lack of representation imply for educational encounters?

Any form of human intersubjectivity would be insignificant without legitimate and suitable representation. Here, we can think of a number of scenarios – from our university classrooms to committees and the faculty. In singling out just one example – that of our classroom in which we teach philosophy of education to students registered for a postgraduate certificate in education (PGCE). The institution where we are based – thanks to apartheid – has a history of privilege in terms of funding, resources and infrastructure. More importantly, it has a history of catering exclusively to white students, as well as white academics and administrators. Despite reform measures brought about by the transition to a democracy more than twenty-five years ago, the kinds of transformation in terms of student and academic demographic transformation that one might have envisaged, or when compared to other historically advantaged universities, has not quite been realised at the university, where we are based. Our PGCE class, for example, is constituted by a predominantly white group of students. In fact, we would go as far as saying that despite the poor representation of the types of diversity encountered in South Africa in our faculty, our representation is remarkably more diverse than the rest of the university. The problem is that when we attempt to discuss issues of diversity, pluralism, multiculturalism, racism or discrimination, the predominant voices who participate in these discussions is that of privilege and a disconnectedness from any form of experienced marginalisation.

Indeed, there have been and are students from historically disadvantaged and minority groups in our class. However, they are neither a critical mass nor adequately representative of the types of communities and learners our PGCE students are likely to encounter as they embark first on their teaching practice, followed by potential teaching positions in South African schools. As teachers, we often find that we have to speak on behalf of those who are not present and not represented. Admittedly, we recognise that our own worldviews and life experiences do not necessarily do justice to the particular experiences of most minority students in our university or our society. In other words, we recognise that as we attempt to sensitise our PGCE students to the reality of different life-worlds and perspectives, we might inadvertently misrecognise those very life-worlds.

Hence, the absence of or a lack of representation would deem human subjects as unworthy of moral and political interaction because misrecognising such humans through underrepresentation are to be remiss of their just potential contribution to public morality and political agency. If underrepresentation were to be present, questions about the good life and just political morality would not be resolved on the basis that human agency would have become privatised, hidden and repressed (Benhabib, 1994: 93). The point is, under-representation would undermine the communicative ethic needed in the pursuit of educational encounters. Consequently, underrepresentivity produces an approach to communicative ethics that does not consider others' rights and responsibilities as public matters to be enacted. Instead, humans' under-representation allows one to dismiss all people's relationality according to their multiple identities and unique individualities. For once, the practice of discourses becomes an impossibility because commonality and uniqueness are not considered as worthy of some form of generalised shared socialisation and the contingency of individual life-histories (Benhabib, 1994: 94). In the main, under-representation is in itself a silencing of people's voices that seriously undermines our fellow humans as generalised and concrete others. The upshot is that education would not just be impeded, but it becomes acutely impossible to pursue.

RECLAIMING REPRESENTATION

Can a post-critical theory of education make a claim for representation more pronounced? It is not unsurprising that Jurgen Habermas (1984) avoids any discussion about gender in *The Theory of Communicative Action*, which, by implication, is a serious deficiency (Fraser, 1994: 32). Nancy Fraser (1994: 44) highlights the conceptual dissonance between and the dialogical capacities central to Habermas's (1984) notion of citizenship. According to Fraser (1994), Habermas's (1984) notion of a critical theory wrongly assumes that citizenship defends the polity and protects women, children and the elderly, who allegedly cannot protect themselves – an idea of critical consciousness that introduces further dissonance into women's relation to citizenship (Fraser, 1994: 44). Moreover, argues Fraser (1990: 63), in many contexts, women and men of racialised ethnicities of all classes are excluded on racial grounds (Fraser, 1990: 63). Therefore, the concerns of access, unendangered mobility and unconstrained deliberation have to be considered concerning unequal access, participation and exclusion. In stratified societies, Fraser (1990: 64) contends, 'Unequally empowered social groups tend to develop unequally valued cultural styles'. The result, she continues, 'is the development of powerful informal pressures that marginalize the contributions of members of subordinated groups both in everyday life contexts and in official public spheres' (Fraser, 1990: 64).

Considering that critical theory, following Habermas (1984), accords citizenship a male-dominated role, it makes sense to look at post-critical theory, specifically poststructuralist thought, to respond to the gender-blindness of Habermas's (1984) critical theory. We now turn to the seminal work of Jacques Derrida to find some way how poststructuralism advances a gender-based form of citizenship – one that enhances the subject of representation.

Jacques Derrida (2004: 153–154) offers an account of representation that stands to produce something or somebody's views, conflicts, contradictions, play and differences beyond the profound and the radical towards thinking that requires reason and going beyond reason towards risks. Suppose one considers that university education is central to Derrida's representation framework, then in a Derridian way. In that case, representing an account of education involves exercising one's freedom to provoke one and others to think and act towards that which is not yet. The double movement of representation is articulated as follows: education is supposed to be a representation of society, and in turn, society reflects on and thinks about education based on renewed understandings taking the university as an institution of education towards that which is still in becoming (Derrida, 2004: 152). If one looks at such an idea of representation, then it follows that educational encounters ought to manifest as follows: First, encounters ought to be stimulated by thinking, deliberation and provocation. The university has to be a space where nothing is beyond interrogation and where all voices are considered. The university, states Derrida (2004: 97),

> is there to tell the truth, to judge, to criticise in the most rigorous sense of the terms, namely to discern and decide between the true and the false; and if it is also entitled to decide between the just and the unjust, the moral and the immoral, this is so insofar as reason and freedom of judgment (that is, risk) are implicated in it as well.

If this is indeed the case, then truth can only emerge when most, if not all, perspectives are taken into account.

If thinking is absent, the educational encounter will fail in its responsibility to provoke deliberation and suspicion among participants. Second, educational encounters guided by thinking would risk taking initiatives towards the future. That is, through thinking and deliberative engagement with others, there is a greater likelihood of considering new ideas to shift outwards towards that which is unknown and unfamiliar. And, if participants were not to be present in encounters, such encounters will not provoke students and teachers to undertake new analyses as they would not be in a position to draw out the possible consequences of their questioning. Teachers are well aware of the latter – they know that if managed correctly in terms of inviting learners or students to participate in classroom discussions and debates – that there is a greater chance of an enlarged and extended discussion and debate, and hence a greater chance of considering matters anew.

Third, education underscored by representation and vice versa would not produce a community of thinking subjected to reason and risks university education becoming occasions 'for silent, paralytic deliberation' where nothing new and useful might be imminent (Derrida, 2004: 132). Thus, if representation were to be misconstrued, the possibility is always there that university education would not just be impeded but also that the university would have shut its eyes to reason and responsibility. This brings us to a discussion about how education will manifest in institutions if it does not deny representation as a legitimate and necessary practice?

First, educational encounters will be ethical. That is, humility towards all others will be exercised, which Drucilla Cornell (1992: 177) describes as showing 'humility before the otherness of the Other'. The point is, educational encounters will inspire to enact ethical relationships through respect for the other. This has implications for how human dialogues unfold that are inherently connected to representative selves. Put differently, dialogues among humans will manifest that undergoes ethical alterity in the sense that all agents in the educational encounters will be recognised. For instance, a woman or man in their otherness cannot be subjected to a gender hierarchy of masculine superiority 'in which the feminine is pushed under' (Cornell, 1992: 180). Second, educational encounters framed according to representation cannot involve the violation of autonomous individuals. For Derrida, there is always the possibility of reconstruction through educational encounters, referred to by Cornell (1992: 181) as 'the possibility of redemption'. In other words, educational encounters should be subjected to renewing things or looking at things anew – that is, the possibility of reconstruction.

Classroom engagements provide numerous and substantive opportunities for learners, students and teachers to stop, pause and think about what they think they know, how they have come to know what they know, and how what they know might not be the only knowledge worth having. One of us recalls one particular PGCE student who was older than his peers and had decided to enter the teaching profession after spending several years as a lawyer. He regularly participated in class discussions, but his inputs were often somewhat problematic because they created moments of uncomfortability for minority group students, in particular. Most of his contributions departed from the premise of a 'proud Afrikaner', who was especially proud of his heritage and language. By themselves, such statements are necessarily problematic. But, within particular contexts and discussions on discrimination and oppression as put into disturbing play by apartheid, his comments could not simply be taken at face-value. Furthermore, while there were one or two students prepared to challenge him on his views on apartheid, his presence and confidence in debate made it difficult not only for him to listen to others' views but also for others to want to engage with him in debate. As aptly articulated by a normally quiet black female student, 'It's as if you don't even see me when you speak to me'.

The moment of redemption coincided with the conclusion of the academic year – just after the students had returned from their six weeks of teaching practice. After being unusually quiet for about six classes, he responded to a particular question by referring to his teaching practice. Evidently, the school where he had been was quite diverse, and by his own account, forced him to interact with learners from a range of backgrounds, races and religions – not only in the classroom but as a rugby coach as well. His greatest learning, he attested, was the realisation that 'they were not what he thought they were'. There was no need for anyone to ask him what exactly he thought they were.

His comments, though subtle, throughout the year, had provided enough insights into his perspectives on race and racial discrimination. Whether or not this moment was a fleeting one, we cannot know. Nevertheless, the moment occurred and confirmed the educational encounter's power as a medium of alterity and transcendence.

As aptly put by Cornell (1992: 181), an educational encounter constituted in representation 'simply demands that we think about the status of the [political] project of reconstruction differently'. Eeducational encounters framed according to the notion of representation should be biased towards justice. Coupled with the idea of cultivating justice, Cornell (1992: 181) posits that human relations should 'give form to the hope of reconciliation . . . and its relation to law'. Here we specifically think of the Truth and Reconciliation Commission (TRC) in South Africa spearheaded by Archbishop Desmond Tutu in the 1990s and early 2000s that extended justice to hope in reconciliation among perpetrators and victims of political and moral violence during apartheid South Africa. While not without criticism for not bringing many perpetrators to justice for their heinous crimes, the TRC managed to create a space where shattered lives and unfound bodies could be brought to life (albeit fractured) through dialogue and hope for a future of reconciled and peaceful coexistence among South Africans.

In sum, under-representation is dangerous to any form of legitimate education. This is so on the grounds that representation creates conditions for ethical, political and juridical significance that can push educational encounters to their limits. In the words of Cornell (1992: 175), humans cannot become automatons as we take up our positions in educational encounters constituted by representation. Educational encounters, as public encounters, need listening to and engaging with the lived experiences and perspectives of all humans. Through this engagement and being in the presence of others, understanding and respect are cultivated and guarded as a foundational premise of democratic citizenship.

Chapter 8

Why Representation Matters in Teaching and Learning

INTRODUCTION

Generally, the dominant debates on minority-group access, representation and participation have primarily been centred on learners or students. The value of cultivating diverse spaces of learning resides not only in engaging with different ways of thinking and being but certainly in widening the scope of learner experience and the capacity to cross over into different perspectives. Moreover, diverse and pluralist educational settings provide both the potential climate and content for learners and students to learn how *to be* with others, as opposed to simply learning *about* others. Comparatively speaking, the same level of attention – certainly not in South Africa – has not been given to the representivity of a diverse teaching community in either schools or universities. To us – as will be unpacked in this chapter – the incongruencies which often emerge between learner or student demographics and teacher representivity (reflective of society) hold particular implications and consequences for teaching and learning. To this end, we will show that the representivity of diverse teaching and learning communities – if managed correctly – have the potential to enhance both teaching and learning and cultivate the spaces necessary for constructive dissensus for the purposes of understanding and respect of difference.

TEACHER (UNDER)REPRESENTATION IN SCHOOLS

Debates and concerns about the underrepresentation of teachers from minority groups are not new. In the United States, for example, it has been an issue of national importance, with numerous scholars and commentators arguing that there is a growing mismatch between the degree of racial/ethnic diversity of the school learner demography and the teaching corps (Ingersoll et al.,

2019). According to Ingersoll et al. (2019: 3), there are three related arguments why, on the one hand, this mismatch is detrimental and, on the other hand, why increasing the racial/ethnic diversity of the teaching force would be beneficial. The first focus on demographic parity is that minority teachers are important as role models for minority and nonminority students. Here the underlying assumption is that the racial/ethnic composition of the teaching corps should reflect that of the student population and that of the larger society (Ingersoll et al., 2019). The second argument, referred to as 'cultural synchronicity', holds that minority-group learners benefit from being taught by minority-group teachers because, state Ingersoll et al. (2019: 3), minority-group teachers are likely to have 'insider knowledge' due to similar life experiences and cultural backgrounds. A third related argument, according to Ingersoll et al. (2019), concerns teacher shortages in disadvantaged schools, which contends that not only are minority-group teachers well-suited to teach minority-group learners, but they are also likely to be motivated by a 'humanistic commitment' to making a difference in the lives of disadvantaged learners. Moreover, minority-group teachers are more likely than nonminority candidates to seek employment in schools serving predominantly minority groups, often located in low-income school districts.

Other arguments in support of a need to increase the racial and cultural diversity of the teacher workforce in the United States, according to Achinstein et al. (2010: 71), is that of a 'demographic imperative' to counter the disparity between the racial and cultural backgrounds of learners and teachers and address concerns about a predominantly white teaching workforce. Moreover, a 'democratic imperative' highlights schools' failure to serve minority-group learners' educational needs (Achinstein et al., 2010). Similar to the 'humanistic commitment' (Ingersoll et al., 2019), some assumptions behind the 'democratic imperative' is that minority-group teachers may be suited to teaching minority-group learners because of a potential understanding of the cultural experiences of these learners and the possibility of promoting culturally responsive teaching, supporting cultural synchronicity and building cultural bridges from home to school for learners (Achinstein et al., 2010: 72).

Proponents of the 'democratic imperative', according to Achinstein et al. (2010: 72), cite an emerging body of research, which suggests that minority-group teachers can produce more favourable academic results on standardised test scores, attendance, retention, advanced-level course enrollment and college-going rates for minority-group learners than white colleagues. Often because of personal experiences with culturally disconnected curriculum or the underresourced conditions of their own schooling, asserts Kohli and Pizarro (2016: 74), minority-group teachers have a heightened awareness of educational injustice and racism. In comparison with 'white' teachers, minority-group teachers have more positive views of minority-group learners, including more favourable perceptions of their academic potential and higher expectations of their learning potential (Kohli & Pizarro, 2016: 74). Moreover, according to Kohli and Pizarro (2016: 74), many minority-group teachers enter the teaching profession with an orientation towards justice and equity – that is, they choose to become teachers because they want to improve the academic experiences of minority-group learners to support the educational transformation of their own communities.

Following this, it is important to note the point made by Achinstein et al. (2010: 72) that advocates for increasing diversity in the teacher workforce. Demographic and democratic imperatives do not claim that white teachers cannot be effective teachers of minority-group learners; employment segregation should be promoted, or that all minority-group teachers are effective with minority-group learners. Proponents do, however, maintain that the demographic discrepancy between the racial and cultural backgrounds of teachers and learners may contribute to the democratic failure to provide students of colour with opportunities to learn (Achinstein et al., 2010: 72).

As a result of these various factors, assert Ingersoll et al. (2019: 4), a lack of minority teacher role models, insufficient cultural synchronicity between teachers and minority students, and a general dearth of qualified teachers in disadvantaged schools, commentators and researchers have concluded that the minority teacher shortage has resulted in unequal access to adequately qualified teachers and, hence, to quality teaching in poor public schools serving minority-group learners. In turn, continue Ingersoll (2019: 4), unequal access to educational resources, such as qualified teachers, has long been considered a primary cause of the stratification of educational opportunity and, in turn, the achievement gap and, ultimately, unequal occupational outcomes for disadvantaged populations.

THE CASE OF SOUTH AFRICA

In South Africa, the post-apartheid institutional desegregation of schools was welcomed with expectations of open schools, social mobility and inclusion. Given the huge gaps regarding resources, infrastructure and learner-to-teacher ratios, learners' migratory patterns from historically disadvantaged (black) schools to historically advantaged (white) schools were inevitable. While schools, historically categorised as 'coloured' and 'Indian', have also experienced an influx of 'black' learners, with the result of an entire shift in learner demographics at some schools, 'black' schools have mainly remained homogeneous in terms of race. What has happened at 'black' schools is the enrolment of significant numbers of learners from foreign African countries.

Teacher migratory patterns from historically 'black' to historically 'white' schools are often based on similar reasons to those of learners, namely better-resourced schools, smaller classes, more opportunities, safer school environments, more learning support services and, in some cases, a higher salary, augmented through the SGB (Davids & Waghid, 2015).

Teacher migratory patterns, however, have been significantly less than that of learners. On the one hand, one finds that most teachers continue to seek employment in schools, which are aligned to their historical racial category. That is, the majority of 'white' teachers continue to seek employment in historically 'white' schools, while 'coloured', 'Indian' and 'black' teachers continue to teach in schools, which they would have attended as learners. On the other hand, even where schools have shifted entirely in their learner demographics, the teacher body does not necessarily reflect this change – with the historical composition and look often remaining intact. For example, several historically categorised 'coloured' or 'Indian' schools have shifted to have 'black' learners as their majority group. Despite these dramatic shifts in learner demographics, this shift is not evident in the teacher demographics. In some cases, the teaching staff will still reflect the original historical racial categorisation of the school. Therefore, it is not unusual to find diverse school environments in terms of learner demographics taught by a teacher corps, which does not reflect this diversity.

There are many complex reasons for the fact that, in most instances, schools in South Africa have managed to retain their historical identities in terms of race and/or ethnicity. Adding to these complexities is a dearth of research that could be ascribed to two reasons. First, is the relative newness of desegregated schools since the introduction of democracy in 1994. Second, is the sensitivities and difficulties associated with this type of research, not only in terms of getting principals to participate in discussions on issues of race and teacher diversity but also in terms of the reluctance of minority-group teachers to disclose experiences of marginalisation or exclusion when they teach in schools where they are not part of a majority group. What we do know – via anecdotal accounts and through conversations with teachers within contexts of other research projects, which might look at teacher identity and professionalism – is that minority-group teachers are kept at bay from historically white schools through subtly disguised forms of rhetoric. The most common form or language is that of 'standards' – there is seemingly an associated fear that employing teachers other than white at historically 'white' schools implies a drop in 'standards'.

Schools have their own predefined 'standards' to justify profound racialised conceptions of a diametrically opposed 'white' competence and 'black' incompetence (Soudien & Sayed, 2004; Walker, 2005). While 'white' teachers possess inherent competencies to teach, 'black', 'coloured' or

'Indian' teachers do not. Notably, while the practice of using 'standards' to exclude minority-group teachers might be especially prevalent at historically 'white' schools, this practice is not limited to 'white' schools. Historically categorised 'coloured' and 'Indian' schools would be reluctant to employ 'black' teachers, but not so about 'white' teachers. Moreover, 'black' schools appoint 'white' principals, while 'coloured' schools refuse to appoint 'black' principals (Makhetha, 2017; Simelane, 2017). The use of 'standards' is worth further consideration; it is used with disturbing comfort by teachers and parents. Just recently, one of us attended a school meeting involving parents, SGB members and the teaching staff, as well as the principal. Inputs from various SGB members, teachers and parents gave the impression that the school had made significant strides towards 'transformation' and cultivated an 'inclusive school environment. Suggestions that the school should take stock on ensuring that its diversity is as prevalent among its teaching staff as it is among learners were met with the standard response of 'standards'. According to its advocates, 'standards' are not racist; 'standards' are necessary to maintain the 'ethos' of a school. Moreover, if the school 'transforms too soon' by employing teachers from diverse groups and identities, there is a risk that 'white' parents would remove their children from the school.

To any reasonable person, and in most contexts, this type of exchange could only be labelled what it is: racism. Not in this case – this is what a post-apartheid society sounds like – so deep are the entrenchments of racialised views of knowledge, skills, competencies and human worth that those who propagate this kind of rhetoric are incapable of seeing for what it is. The depth and harm are such that even 'black' teachers believe that they are less capable, less competent and less knowledgeable. One of us had to attend a 'meet-your-child's teacher' – a common practice at the commencement of academic school years. The homeroom or class teacher was a 'black' female – a highly unusual encounter in a historically white school. Generally, when historically 'white', 'coloured' or 'Indian' schools employ 'black' teachers, it is to teach Xhosa, never as a class teacher. The surprise of encountering this anomaly was soon dampened when the group of parents (predominantly white) who had gathered in the classroom to meet with the teacher were, in fact, addressed by the grade head – a 'white' female. She explained that she would be addressing the parents instead, because she was the science teacher and taught all of the learners in this class, whereas the class teacher did not teach all of the learners in her class and only saw all of the learners briefly during the morning session. Throughout the time that 'white' grade head spoke to parents, the 'black' teacher stood quietly in the corner – occasionally nodding as she was called upon to confirm this or the other.

It is unclear whether this situation made anyone else in the room feel uncomfortable, but one of us decided to raise the matter privately with the 'black' teacher a few days later to ascertain why she, as the class teacher, had not spoken to parents, as was the practice in other classrooms. She responded that she had asked the grade head to address parents – she had experienced anxiety just thinking about it and hoped to be more confident the following year. She provided an assurance that her anxiety did not extend to learners, only to parents. Of course, it might be the case that the teacher was indeed anxious, that she preferred talking to learners over parents. However, it is hard to ignore the fact that this is not a newly qualified or inexperienced teacher – why would she have anxiety about addressing a group of parents? The answer lies in an intersectional mess of apartheid oppression and dehumanisation – so successful that a qualified 'black' teacher', who must have impressed via her CV and her interview to get a post at a historically white school in the first place, feels too intimidated address the parents of learners whom she teaches.

Commonly, 'black' teachers are excluded from historically 'white' schools through a language of 'standards', which is used as an alternative to exclusion based on race, culture or ethnicity. Often, these standards are vague and undefined; they exist in some kind of normative realm of how teaching ought to unfold and, more importantly, who ought to be teaching (Davids, 2019). It is not that a 'black' teacher is less qualified or less knowledgeable than a 'white' colleague. Instead, who the 'black' teacher is, and what they bring is perceived to be different and, hence, of no value. In this regard, the use of 'standards', therefore, should not be understood as a judgement of excellence; it is about fitting in and assimilating to a preexisting norm of being and acting.

According to Kohli and Pizarro (2016: 73), attempts by teachers from diverse backgrounds to bring their identities into an existing ethos or their profession are met with resistance, which makes it difficult for them to engage holistically with their colleagues and learners. It is not only the diverse backgrounds of minority-group teachers but their knowledge that is constituted through their identities – the kind of knowledge that would raise questions about their 'competence' and 'standards'. One finds, at times, that resistance to teachers from minority groups is reframed and justified in terms of pedagogical access by learners. A South African 'Indian' teacher, appointed at a 'white' school, continually had to face parents' complaints that their children could not understand his accent. After only ten months at the school, his decision to leave was made when the principal asked him whether he would be taking leave to celebrate Eid (a Muslim festival day). The principal had seemingly failed to realise that he was, in fact, not Muslim but a practising Hindu – raising all sorts of questions about essentialised constructions and conceptions of identity and cultural orientation (Davids & Waghid, 2015). Even when teachers are externally included, their pedagogic authority is brought into disrepute through questions of 'competence' and 'standards'. One such example involves a 'black' teacher, who was appointed at a 'coloured' school as a teacher of Mathematics but was only allowed to teach Mathematical Literacy on the basis that she required 'mentoring'. Four years after being appointed, she was still teaching only Mathematical Literacy (Davids & Waghid, 2015).

In sum, South African schools, although desegregated, have yet to depart from paradigms from segregated thinking. Often the allowance of access to learners from diverse backgrounds is precisely that – an allowance – a criterion that needs to be adhered to so as to avoid being forced to do so by educational authorities. Generally, historically advantaged (white) schools predecide the number of learners from diverse groups they intend to accept each academic year. This is by no means an organic process of accepting learners based on their application. This process involves intense scrutiny of racial identity, followed by that of class.

Moreover, thanks to a particular funding structure and policy – the National Norms and Standards for School Funding (NNSSF) (DoE, 1998) – schools are classified into wealth quintiles (1–5) and subsidised accordingly. Schools serving more impoverished communities must receive more state funding than schools serving better-off communities. The NNSSF (DoE, 1998) forms part of a range of post-apartheid policies geared at the government's efforts to redress historical imbalances and achieve equity in public schools. Although laudable in terms of its social justice imperative, schools the NNSSF (DoE, 1998), together with the South African Schools Act (DoE, 1996), allows SGB's to determine the school fees at their respective schools. Hence, one finds that 'wealthier' – generally, historically 'white' schools – receive the lowest state subsidy (as to be expected), but as a result, escalate their school fees in order not only to cover the shortfall created by a low subsidy but to sustain their historical advantage. Schools are under tremendous pressure to ensure that the learners, whom they let through their doors, have parents who can pay the fees. As a result, schools continue to be segregated along economic lines, which invariably translates into racial lines, given historical privilege's residual effects.

We continue this chapter by turning our attention to what it means to be present and represented as an act of recognition.

TOWARDS REPRESENTATION AS PRESENCE AND INCLUSION

According to a theory on representationalism/representation, we directly access ideas that represent the world, not the world itself. Such a theory of representation has been debunked by Richard Rorty (1988), who claims that representation is of no point and that it is enough to accept justified beliefs as true knowledge. We are more interested in a different view of representivity – that is, one that speaks to a notion of re-present in the sense that being present is recurring. The point is, representation is about being present over and over again. So, the idea of representivity we envisage to examine concerning being engaged in human encounters is a notion that speaks to being present always, in this instance, educational encounters. And, for elucidation on this notion of always being present, we once again turn to the seminal thoughts of Axel Honneth and Jacques Rancière (2016). In this way, we argue that representivity matters.

Following Honneth and Rancière (2016) seminal ideas on a theory of recognition, they accentuate two aspects of recognition: first, when we recognise something (a place, a person, a situation or an argument), we do so based on the knowledge we already possess. When a teacher recognises a student, the teacher does so based on having some prior knowledge of who the student is. A teacher would not be in a position to recognise a student without some knowledge of who the student is or what the student does. Second, recognition means 'that we respond to the claim of other individuals who demand that we treat them as autonomous entities or equal persons' (Honneth & Rancière, 2016: 84). Moreover, when we treat people as autonomous and equal persons, we recognise that 'they construct, even through struggle, relations of confidence, respect, and esteem with other people' – that is, to take responsibility for them (Honneth & Rancière, 2016: 86). Yet, accounting for others implies that one recognises others to be there – that is, to be present. The point we are making is that recognition is inextricably linked to the notion of representation. If one were not to be present, how else would one be recognised?

Conversely, if one recognises someone, that person must be present. Differently put, recognition and representation are inextricably linked. So, a Honneth and Rancierean conception of recognition seems to be open to a notion of representation. It is this connection between recognition and representation that creates spaces of play and alterations. In other words, following Honneth and Rancière (2016: 89), there is space for a 'becoming other' in the very conformation of what it means to be in the presence of another. Therefore, representation is a matter of affirming the presence of an other who can undergo an 'alterity' (Honneth & Rancière, 2016: 89).

Let us illustrate the aforementioned discussion with a pedagogical example. A teacher recognises that her students or learners have the capability to learn if they are introduced to a subject matter with which the teacher is familiar. That is, a teacher is knowledgeable about her subject and, on this basis, invites her students to learn. What inspires the teacher to teach is that she knows something about her learners or students and their capacities to learn.

The teacher passionately teaches as she recognises her students' ability to learn. On the grounds of her knowledge about a particular subject matter and her passionate teaching, she manages to open up her students' minds about the subject. And, for the latter to happen, teachers recognise not only their students' capabilities but also their presence as they disclose their knowledge to their students. What is even more significant about the teaching of a passionate and knowledgeable teacher is the recognition that students can learn or what Honneth and Rancière (2016: 93) refers to as their 'equal capacity to discuss common affairs . . . [and] enacting it'.

When learners or students learn, they demonstrate their ability to speak for themselves independently, which implies that they affirm their presence through their learning. The upshot of learning in the present, following Honneth and Rancière (2016: 146–147), 'is the affirmation of their [students'] capacity to reconstruct their world of experience, therefore to take their part in the global configuration of the social world . . . [in which] they allow for new possibilities of collective enunciation'. Our interest in opening up new possibilities resulting from being present is related to Honneth and Rancière's (2016: 155) idea of dissensus. For him, when humans are in the presence of others, they recognise one another's equality and their capacities for dissensus or disagreement. This has to be so; otherwise, why would humans engage with one another in the first place? Dissensus is explained as follows:

> Every situation can be cracked open on the inside, reconfigured in a different regime of perception and signification, *altering the landscape of what can be seen and what can be thought*, along with the field of the possible and the distribution of capacities and incapacities. (Honneth & Rancière, 2016: 155, italics added)

The upshot of the aforementioned argument is that recognising presence invokes the possibility for dissensus that invariably works against the domination of one person or group over another person or group. Resisting domination on the grounds of dissensus opens the door for emancipation, argue Honneth and Rancière (2016: 154). In his words, emancipation is 'the construction of new capacities . . . the endless critique of illusions produced by the system of domination' (Honneth & Rancière, 2016: 153). The point we are making is that being in the presence opens up spaces for dissensus to manifest, making emancipatory action possible. This happens when 'there is a capacity for thinking that does not belong to any special group, a capacity than can be attributed to anybody' (Honneth & Rancière, 2016: 150). Thus, recognising the presence of anybody is, in fact, an affirmation that such persons are capable of producing arguments that are relevant to the intelligence of anybody – that is, confirming the equality of persons again.

IMPLICATIONS OF INCLUSION FOR TEACHING AND LEARNING

Following a Honneth and Rancierean approach, teaching and learning should be free from constraints for both teachers and learners or students. In other words, they (teachers and students) should be allowed to exercise their equal intelligence to shape teaching and learning discourse. This renewed freedom of being a liberatory teacher and students has at least the following actions in mind: first, when students and teachers are free, they are also free to criticise. Here, criticism means that teachers and students should bring to light the unrepresented aspects of society, especially those unaccounted for and remain marginalised. Certainly, in South Africa, the implication is that social justice education should be about bringing into presence those aspects of society that remain voiceless – a matter of overcoming injustice.

Second, teaching and learning should become more resistant to forms of domination. In this way, teaching and learning can produce more emancipatory opportunities for both teachers and learners or students. Through an emancipatory discourse of teaching and learning, teachers and students can disrupt unequal pedagogical relations that seem to subvert their equal capacities to enact their freedoms.

Third, teaching and learning imply a commitment to remaining open to all forms of disagreement or dissensus. What should ensue from a pedagogy of dissensus are human relations that alter and ruptures the possible (Honneth & Rancière, 2016: 119). What dissensus has in mind is that teachers construct multiple pathways in terms of which they can explain their points without making predictions. The point is, the teaching of dissensus is without absoluteness, where there remains room for new exchanges and different claims about truth.

In conclusion, ensuring that schools are diverse and have representivity from all sectors of society is imperative not only for learners or students but also for teachers. This is as true in terms of learner representivity as it is in teacher representivity. On the one hand, learners or students learn about how to engage with different ways of thinking and being by actually being in spaces where they can encounter these differences. In this way, their learning is not limited to theoretical discussions and debates; instead, their worldviews are broadened and challenged by others. Much has been written in this chapter about the role and value of minority-group teachers in relation to minority-group learners. However, minority-group teachers can be of similar value to learners who constitute the majority group in schools. By learning from and with a minority-group teacher, learners, who might otherwise never have encountered such a teacher, is awakened to the possibility that it is possible to learn from different people. Commonly, and as is the case in historically 'white' schools in South Africa, divisions between those who teach and those who serve the roles of maintenance and cleaning staff are defined along racial lines. One of the implications is that 'black' people are not assumed to be capable of teaching. Therefore, the presence of a 'black' teacher serves to disrupt this racist stereotype and opens opportunities for new types of learning.

On the other hand, diverse representation and inclusion of learners are critical to teachers' growth and learning. A diverse classroom provides opportunities for teachers to step out of that which is already known to them. More importantly, provided they are open and willing to engage with different perspectives and life-worlds, the presence of diversity facilitates the cultivation of democratic citizenship education. In this sense, teachers do not simply get to talk about democratic citizenship but get to show it and learn from it by ensuring that all learners are recognised and included.

The entire point of schooling and education is to prepare young people for their roles as citizens. Schools cannot shy away from the knowledge and obligation that while schooling is temporary, education is not. Schools ought to provide the space and ethos where democratic practices are not only made visible in the inclusion of diverse learners and teachers but where the very ideals of democratic citizenship – that is, equal recognition, inclusion, respect – are preserved. It matters, therefore, what learners are taught, and it matters who teachers are. Stated differently, young people learn not only by *what* and *how* they are taught, but they also learn from *whom* they are taught. It is often not enough for learners to learn about different ways of being and acting; they have to be able to participate in those differences.

This chapter has argued that teaching and learning should be free from constraints for both teachers and learners or students. In other words, they (teachers and students) should be allowed to exercise their equal intelligence to shape teaching and learning discourse. Second, teaching and learning should become more resistant to forms of domination. In this way, teaching and learning can produce more emancipatory opportunities for both teachers and learners or students. Third, to teach and learn implies a commitment to remaining open to all forms of disagreement or dissensus; what dissensus has in mind is that teachers construct multiple pathways in terms of which they can explain their points without making predictions. Finally, learner or student and teacher diversity can be of equal benefit to all teachers and learners or students and can only expand and enhance educational encounters.

Chapter 9

Reopening Debates about Engagement and Belonging

INTRODUCTION

Much of the debates in and about democratic citizenship education centre around notions of engagement and belonging. Feeling a sense of belonging, we know, can take several forms – from that which is physically manifested and concrete to abstract ways – and varies from person to person. At times, an individual might have a strong sense of belonging, particularly when their particular values or perspectives are confirmed; other times, feeling a sense of belonging might be under major strain, leading to an individual feeling disconnected, unseen and misrecognised. Feeling a sense of belonging is critical to the well-being and recognition of individuals, groups or communities. In educational settings, notions and experiences of belonging adopt added complexities and nuances that may not be immediately evident to teachers or learners or students. Experiencing a sense of belonging is intricately embedded in what it means to be included – that is, to be drawn into the presence and the presence of others. Inclusion, however, exists in a dyadic relationship with exclusion – that is, that inclusion cannot be understood without making sense of that which excludes. Drawing on Jacques Delors's (1996) notion of learning, we offer a different understanding of democratic citizenship education that can contribute towards reshaping notions of inclusion and hence, belonging. In this way, hopefully, we shall respond to racial, ethnic and social exclusions.

INCLUSION/EXCLUSION

Part of the complexities of understanding conceptions and practices of inclusion and exclusion is that it adopts different forms and trajectories within different contexts. Understandings of inclusion and exclusion, explains De Haan (2000), are socially constructed and rooted in the contexts in which they find themselves. The term 'inclusion', state Graham and Slee (2008: 278), implies a particular centredness, a pre-existing discursive space; it 'implies a *bringing in*' (Graham, 2006: 20), 'in that it presupposes a whole into which something (or someone) can be incorporated' (Graham & Slee, 2008: 278). Already, following Graham and Slee (2008), one immediately becomes aware of a subconscious text, or worldview, some sort of pre-existing agreement. This presupposes not only an already established space of inclusion and inclusiveness but 'a *bringing in*' (Graham, 2006: 20), which suggests that an individual cannot simply presume to be included; instead 'a *bringing in*' needs to take place. This inclusive space presumes particular taken-for-granted norms, which, by virtue of inclusion, accords a sense of belonging to some, but possibly not all. This is because, as Graham (2006: 8) explains, the 'norm' produces a particular reality – 'It produces domains through normative discursive practices that affirm or negate particular ways of being'.

As the term 'inclusion' arguably presupposes the already begun, Graham and Slee (2008: 279) questions whether the term 'inclusive' is less likely to bring about the sense of foreclosure that appears inherent to inclusion. What 'normative circuitry may we be drawing on to do this and what circuit breakers might we deploy to avoid' doing so, asks Graham and Slee (2008: 280). Although this pre-existing space of inclusion is predicated as natural and true, explain Graham and Slee (2008: 282), the rule of the norm is statistically derived, negating the diversity to be found within the nature and naturalness of diversity. Therefore, one finds that while exclusion is generally a consequence of attitudes and responses to race, social, class, ethnicity, religion, gender and ability, the shifting trajectories imply the risk of a ubiquitous exclusion (Peters & Besley, 2014: 109). This means that it is impossible to have a clear sense of who, how and when someone might be excluded, but that the inclusion of an individual does not negate the potential of any exclusion.

To request inclusion, asserts Stiker (1999: xxi), 'is to underscore one's desire for assimilation into a norm. . . . A community's marginality is implicitly underscored by the request for inclusion itself'. As such, he calls for an examination of the different forms of social inclusion. To Stiker (1999: 16–17),

> The dilemma, exclude or include, hides a whole series of exclusions that are not all the same and of inclusions which are not all commensurate. We could

just as well say that the dilemma is illusory. What are societies doing when they exclude in one way or another and when they integrate in this fashion or that? What do they say about themselves in so doing? The study of everything that we call the marginalized allows us to bring out previously ignored or neglected dimensions of that society. Even more: these are indicators of social and cultural dynamics. That is, they testify not so much to where society is going as to the tensions that are resident in it.

Conceptions of inclusion, therefore, do not infer a preclusion of exclusion. The binary of inclusion/exclusion, according to Peters and Besley (2014: 100), is 'a horizontal segmentalization that intimates spatial metaphors detailing marginalization, segregation, confinement and scientification or the production of scientific objectivity through architectures of the gaze, including the model of the panopticon'. With this binary, continue Peters and Besley (2014: 101), is also a realisation of processes of naturalisation and social construction that discursively created human beings as subjects or nonsubjects, as human or something less than human; as abnormal. The binary of inclusion/exclusion, however, does not necessarily imply a horizontal delineation. That is, the idea of inclusion does not stand in opposition to exclusion, in the same way that the gaze of the panopticon is not only horizontal. Unlike horizontal lines that never cross each other, inclusion can intersect with exclusion.

For this reason, Young (2000) maintains that inclusion does not necessarily equate to inclusive processes of recognition, participation or respect. The external inclusion of people does not mean that they are included in the internal interplay of power relations. Stated differently, a legitimate right to inclusion does not preclude other vectors of exclusion and marginalisation. Those who are already within the functioning of power might allow others in, but that does not mean that the power relation ceases (Davids, 2019). One finds, therefore, that although a teacher might be appointed at a particular school – thereby being granted external inclusion – internal exclusion can persist through systemic practices, which are held in place through uncontested realms of power (Davids, 2019).

For this reason, Graham and Slee (2007: 281) contend that limited notions and models of inclusion, such as those realised through resourcing mechanisms that ensure the objectivisation of individual difference, result not only in an ever more complex and insidious exclusion but arguably work to refine schooling as a field of application for disciplinary power. To this end, as contended by Graham and Slee (2007: 280), perhaps, the question is not so much how we move 'toward inclusion', but rather what we need to do in order to disrupt the construction of the centre from which exclusion derives. It is imperative, maintains Graham (2006: 21), that we move beyond limiting notions of inclusion that seek to incorporate 'recognised' forms of otherness within a reified mainstream and to instead develop an inclusive ecology that caters to all through the shared understanding that diversity and multiple ways of being are in fact 'the norm' (Graham, 2006: 21).

INCLUSION AS BELONGING

Appiah (2006: 5) explains that people are making up and drawing from a vast collection of identities to live in the modern world because identities are so diverse. Teachers, for example, have multiple identities that connect them to an array of other identities – such as race, gender, religion, ethnicity, culture, sexuality, as well as marital status, type of family, interests, and political views. Teachers, like all other individuals, therefore, are never just one identity and depending on the context in which they find – at school, at home or their place of worship – and depending on their sense of inclusion in these contexts, they shift in how they respond to those around them. Mendieta (2008: 407) describes identity as being constructed, invented, imagined, imposed, projected and as a 'social locus' of how an individual positions herself within a particular context. Depending on how an individual negotiates the particular influences of his or her 'social locus' – whether imaginary or not – the social space, states Mendieta (2008: 412), is continually shifting and transforming. To him, if a constantly changing 'social topography influences identity', then identities have to be understood as 'fragile negotiations' with their respective 'social topography' (Mendieta, 2008: 412).

In this respect, teachers, who feel excluded, unacknowledged or misrecognised by their peers by virtue of their race or ethnicity, might enter into different modes of interactions and engagement with their 'social locus' in order to find a point of resonance and a sense of belonging. This might include assimilation into the dominant ethos – which might involve attempts at minimising the particular aspect of his or her identity, which he or she understands to solicit the most unease or judgement. A 'black' teacher on a majority 'white' staff might feel the need to change his or her accent or even change his or her name so that it might be easier to pronounce or minimise the 'Africanness' of his or her identity. A hijab-wearing Muslim woman might feel uncomfortable about wearing her hijab and might end up removing it to make one aspect of her Islamic identity less visible, thereby hoping for inclusion. Similarly, a gay man might choose to hide his sexual identity for fear of being labelled or suspected of paedophilia. One way of harmoniously addressing all these divergent identities (Appiah, 2006: 5) is by valuing them, instead of perceiving them as potential limitations, and therefore excluding them. And here, we believe, Appiah's (2006) approach is as much directed at the individual as it is at others. In other words, while it is reasonable to expect others to accept as organic and multifaceted identities, with our own values, beliefs and perspectives, it is equally reasonable to expect that we value our unique characteristics so that we do not feel that ashamed about them, or feel compelled to repress that which distinguishes from others. Other times, and on the other end of the spectrum, minority-group teachers might feel so unseen or insecure that they consciously choose to self-exclude by not participating or engaging or resisting the status quo. In other words, they refuse to play into the pre-existing norms that dictate how they ought to be and behave.

In turn, Appiah (2006: 6) cautions against assuming that previously excluded groups are automatically seeking recognition just because they are seeking new social practices in order to flourish. Often, when new teachers or learners come into a school, which they might have been prohibited from teaching at before – as was the case during apartheid. The presumption by the majority group is that the new teachers or learners want to be a part of, and want to be included in the ways and ambit of the dominant group. But, as is Appiah's (2006) argument, this is not always the case. Not every individual or group are seeking to be included or feel a need to belong. We find this in our own faculty, where certain academics contain their focus only on their work; they refuse to participate in the university's institutional culture and practices because they remain cognisant of the university's role in the propagation of apartheid. Not all political claims, made in the name of a group identity, argues Appiah (2006: 6), are primarily claims for recognition. He expounds that because identities are composed in part by norms of identification and by treatment, there is no plain distinction between recognition and a new kind of oppression, 'If recognition involves taking notice of one's identity in social life, then the development of strong norms of identification can become not liberating but oppressive' (Appiah, 2006: 6). In agreement, Benhabib (2002) asserts that struggles for recognition are, in fact, attempts to counteract the status of otherness insofar as the latter is assumed to entail disrespect and inequality.

Following the preceding discussion and taking the concept of belonging into account, Yuval-Davis (2011: 12) differentiates between three major analytical facets in which belonging is constructed and interrelated but cannot be reduced to each other. The first facet of social locations, says Yuval-Davis (2011: 12–13), refers to a particular sex, race, class or nation, age group, kinship group or a certain profession to which people belong. Social locations, she explains, even in their most stable format, are virtually never constructed along one power vector of difference. Teachers, therefore, as a collective, belong to the profession of teaching, but their race, ethnicity or gender might play particular roles in either providing a stronger connection or a strained relationship with their profession. A 'white' female teacher, in a 'white'-dominated school, for example, might enjoy acceptance and privilege by virtue of her racial categorisation, but she might encounter some prejudice concerning her gender. As such, the idea of a shared (teaching) profession does not infer shared experiences. It is entirely plausible and possible for a staff of teachers at the same school to have very different experiences of their colleagues and the way they engage with learners and parents.

The second facet relates to people's identifications and emotional attachments to various collectivities and groupings. For Yuval-Davis (2011: 14), identities are not just personal but also collective, and collective identity narratives provide a collective sense of order and meaning. Crucial to the construction and reproduction of identity narratives and constructions of attachment, she continues, are specific repetitive practices relating to specific social and cultural spaces that link individual and collective behaviour (Yuval-Davis, 2011: 15–16). As such, says Yuval-Davis (2011: 16), identity is not only constructed in dialogue (that is between the individual and others, or the collective), but the dialogical construction of identity is both reflective and constitutive – 'It is not individual or collective, but involves both, in an in-between state of "becoming", in which processes of identity construction, authorisation and contestation take place'. However, problems arise when individuals are led to believe that who they are – in terms of their gender, race, ethnicity, class or sexuality – is considered less than, inferior or unacceptable. In this regard, a 'black' lesbian teacher might be comfortable with her race or ethnicity, gender and sexuality, as an individual but might struggle to find points of acceptance concerning each of her identity markers. She might, for example, enjoy a sense of belonging as a 'black' woman within her own 'black' community, but she might encounter aversion and exclusion concerning her identity as a lesbian. In this sense, as Yuval-Davis (2011: 17) observes, 'all identities are exclusive, as well as inclusive'. Inclusion and exclusion, explains Yuval-Davis (2011: 17), 'is often not mutual, depending on the power positionality and normative values of the social actors as well as, and in relation to their cognitive and emotional identifications'.

The third facet relates to ethical and political value systems with which people judge their own and others' belonging. Belonging, argues Yuval-Davis (2011: 18), is not just about social locations and constructions of individual and collective identities and attachments; it also is concerned with the ways these are assessed and valued by the self and others. What matters here is how an individual conceives his or her identity in relation to the self and the collective. Constructions of the self and identity, says Yuval-Davis (2011: 18), can, in certain historical contexts, be forced on people. Here again, apartheid provides a chillingly appropriate example – anyone, who was not classified as 'white', was led to believe that their ensuing oppression and inferiority were due to their skin colour. Whatever aspirations they might have as human beings would necessarily be curtailed, and at times, prohibited by virtue of their skin colour. Unsurprisingly, many 'black' people continue to believe in their own less-than, subjugated status; they experience great difficulty embracing who they are and asserting their particular identity. It is evident in some elderly 'black' people in South Africa, who unconsciously bow their heads, avoid eye contact and hands folded in submission as they address 'white' individuals, even when those individuals are children. In other words, they have succumbed to the misguided misrecognition through which they were constructed and relegated by apartheid and its unashamed racism. People's particular histories do not only construct their life stories, their perspectives and perceptions of themselves and others, but their histories might serve as inadvertent barriers to whom they might otherwise have become.

TOWARDS A RENEWED UNDERSTANDING OF LEARNING AND ITS RAMIFICATIONS FOR DEMOCRATIC CITIZENSHIP EDUCATION

To begin with, it was the British philosopher Gilbert Ryle who elucidated the concepts of 'knowing how' and 'knowing that' in the exercise of the human mind (Ryle, 2007: 14). For Ryle (2007: 17) to know how to perform tasks is dependent on people's competencies to do so. In his words:

> We speak of learning how to play an instrument as well as of learning that something is the case; of finding out how to prune trees as well as of finding out that the 'Romans had a camp in a certain place'; of forgetting how to tie a reef-knot as well as of forgetting that the German for 'knife' is '*Messer*' (Ryle, 2007: 17).

The point about how to do something is inextricably linked to the understanding one has of that something. In other words, operationalising something must be preceded by an acknowledgement that that something is what it is. A person can only execute something if he knows what ought to be done. That is, a writer cannot write about a subject if she does not have knowledge of the subject. For Ryle (2007: 18), one considers 'appropriate propositions' and puts into practice what these propositions en-join – that is, 'to do a bit of theory and then to do a bit of practice'. The understanding of learning espoused by Ryle (2007) requires one to know this or that and then to put into practice what one knows – a matter of learning how to do.

If one were to link the aforementioned understanding of learning – learning that and learning how to do – to the notion of democratic citizenship education, one first needs to acquire knowledge of democratic citizenship education before one can enact it. This makes sense because one cannot claim to embark on pursuing democratic citizenship without having some understanding of it.

Inasmuch as learning that and learning how have been dominant for many years, since Ryle's (2007) first publication of his, *The Concept of Mind*, these concepts were extended most notably through the work of Jacques Delors (1996) and the Commission on Education for the Twenty-First Century which produced the report, '*Learning: The Treasure Within*', otherwise known as the '*Delors Report*'. The Delors Commission announced that education comprises four principles of learning: learning that, learning how to, learning to be and learning to live together (Delors et al., 1996: 22). In the words of Delors et al. (1996: 18):

> [E]ducation's noble task [is] to encourage each and everyone, acting in accordance with their traditions and convictions and paying full respect to pluralism, to lift their minds and spirits to the plane of the universal and, in some measure, to transcend themselves. It is no exaggeration on the Commission part to say that the survival of humanity depends thereon.

Clearly, Delors et al. (1996) and the Commission of UNESCO – United Nations Educational, Scientific and Cultural Organisation – advance a humanist view of education that not only corroborates the notion of learning that and learning how to but also extends the latter forms of learning to 'learning to be' and 'learning to live together'. As aptly stated by Delors et al. (1996: 22):

> Developing an understanding of others and their history, and traditions and spiritual values and, on this basis creating a new spirit which . . . would induce people to implement common projects or to manage the inevitable conflicts in an intelligent and peaceful way.

Learning to be implies that one can know this or that and, in turn, act upon what one knows, but this does not mean that one actually internalises what one has acquired. For instance, learning about deliberation and advancing the idea of deliberative engagement is different from deliberating. For this reason, the notion of learning to be becomes significant for democratic citizenship education. That is, democratic citizenship education is about acquiring knowledge of the practice and enhancing it in the society and living it.

Of course, the idea of learning that, learning how and learning to be is in opposition to a neoliberal, instrumentalist form of learning that seems to advance the realisation of a common humanity. However, the notion of learning to live together is novel in the sense that education is considered as a way to cultivate a humanity where peace and prosperity can be achieved through diversity and difference. Put differently, learning to live together in diversity and difference and not in unity implies that education would contribute to humans transcending race, ethnicity and gender.

The question arises, what would a reconfigured notion of democratic citizenship education look like? In one of our most recent works, we espouse a notion of democratic citizenship education that seems to be underscored by the following aspects: First, deliberative freedom and co-learning, iterations, belligerent and distressful action complemented by compassionate imagining constitute democratic citizenship education (Davids & Waghid, 2019). The aforementioned are not just an understanding of democratic action that guides an active citizenry but also how democratic action and citizenship ought to manifest – a matter of internalising 'that' and enacting 'how' democratic citizenship education ought to be realised.

Second, and as we enunciate throughout our work, '[democratic] iterations are both rationally and emotionally conceived . . . [and] it would be unjustifiable to delink democratic education from rational articulations and rearticulations and emotional will formation' (Davids & Waghid, 2019: 25). The point about accentuating rational and emotive (re)articulations is based on the premise that humans ought to 'be'; that is, they are not only familiar with the understanding of democratic citizenship education but also know how to execute it and to live it. Third, as we espoused throughout our work, democratic citizenship education does not merely involve knowing what it is, implementing it and living it. Also, democratic citizenship education is fundamentally about cultivating justice in human relations – that is, learning to live together in diversity and difference with mutual respect and compassion for one another (Davids & Waghid, 2019). The aforementioned understanding of democratic citizenship education invokes at least the following aspects of human living: namely, knowing that, knowing how, knowing to be and knowing to live together. It follows, therefore, that democratic citizenship education is about cultivating just action because justice is intertwined with having knowledge of this or that, executing what one knows, living it and living together with others. As we accentuate in our work, '[i]t is, therefore, quite possible to assert that there is always potential for new becomings and new re-beginnings of thought' (Davids & Waghid, 2019: 114), it seems prudent to reconfigure democratic citizenship education.

FRAMING A RECONFIGURED NOTION OF DEMOCRATIC CITIZENSHIP EDUCATION

Based on the aforementioned explication of democratic citizenship education, the concept seems to be constituted by, first, human deliberative engagement;

second, the enactment of iterations in an atmosphere of co-belonging; third, humans' willingness to be attentive to one another's diverse forms of living; and fourth, a recognition that humans should live together peacefully and securely. We want to expand the idea that humans should live together in harmony.

When humans live together peacefully, they recognise one another's civic equality to treat all persons as equal citizens. They (humans) respect the freedom of all persons to live their own lives as they see fit, consistent with others' freedom. Additionally, all persons have an opportunity to live a decent life according to their preference (Gutmann, 2003: 27). Living together in peace implies living with others based on civic equality, equal freedom and equal opportunity (Gutmann, 2003: 27). If democratic citizenship education were to involve exercising one's freedom, equality and opportunity, then the possibility is always there to live together peacefully – that is, democratic living would be possible on ethical grounds. In this regard, Amy Gutmann (2003: 29) argues,

> A just democracy helps secure for all persons the conditions of civic equality, equal freedom, and basic opportunity, principles that are preconditions of a fair democratic process but are also valuable in their own right as expressions of the freedom and equality of individual persons as ethical agents.

A democratic citizenry that respects all persons as free and equal invariably creates opportunities for deliberative engagements about what counts as good human living – that is, a form of living that opposes exploitation, exclusion and discrimination. Of course, living with freedom, equality and opportunity implies 'being free to express one's identity and shape it through one's associations with others' (Gutmann, 2003: 200) – a matter of living together peacefully. Gutmann (2003: 200) cautions that free association has the potential to exclude others and posits 'the right of free association ends where injustice to others begins' (Gutman, 2003: 200). Unjust discrimination on the grounds of gender, race, sexual orientation, ethnicity and religion invariably impede civic equality, equal freedom and opportunity of all individuals (Gutmann, 2003: 200). Such discrimination undermines any form of democratic citizenship and should not be supported. Here, Gutmann (2003: 210) aptly states the following:

> The promise of democratic justice is to grant individuals equal freedom and opportunity to live their lives as they see fit rather than to see their identities writ large in their very own society. This promise is hard to realize, but it is defensible on democratic grounds.

Finally, and by way of example, we examine whether India's new Citizenship Amendment Bill (CAB), passed by its parliament in 2019, complies with the notion of a reconfigured democratic citizenship education agenda? The bill provides citizenship to religious minorities from Pakistan, Bangladesh and Afghanistan. The government, led by the Hindu nationalist Bharatiya Janata Party (BJP), claims this will give sanctuary to people fleeing religious persecution. However, critics assert that the bill is part of a BJP agenda to marginalise Muslims. Furthermore, the bill makes an exception for members of six religious minority communities – Hindu, Sikh, Buddhist, Jain, Parsi and Christian – if they can prove that they are from Pakistan, Afghanistan or Bangladesh, to apply for citizenship on the grounds that they provide proof of having lived or worked in India for six years. The bill, however, excludes Muslims, considered by opponents as exclusionary as it violates the secular principles enshrined in the country's constitution. It is rightly argued that religion cannot become a condition of citizenship. In the first place, excluding persons on the grounds of their faith to possible eligibility for citizenship in the world's largest democracy seems to be an act of discriminating against 115 million Muslims in contemporary India. Second, not considering Muslims as persons who can live together with others would escalate tensions in the country and exclude them from the possibility of co-belonging and prevent them from exercising their constitutional rights. In this sense, the new CAB seems incommensurate with any form of democratic citizenship education.

In summary, we argued that a reconfigured notion of democratic citizenship education could be articulated as follows: First, to publicise what one considers to be important in cultivating a democratic citizenry – that is, to announce the significance of iterations and co-belonging; second, to advance talking back and co-belonging in one's actual societal practices by showing how it is done; third, by expressing outwardly what one has internalised; and fourth, by living together peacefully with others in an atmosphere of mutuality and ethical commitment.

Chapter 10

Democratic Citizenship Education versus Cosmopolitan Education

INTRODUCTION

Many of the arguments in defence of democratic citizenship education relate to enacting democratic human relations in a spirit of co-belonging to the nation-state. One can hardly find criticisms that would take issue with the cultivation of democratic action, the exercise of rights and responsibilities, and a desire to co-belong in an atmosphere of mutuality and respect. Yet, one aspect of human living does not come easily with just a focus on democratic citizenship education: attentiveness to the other in its otherness. To act democratically implies engaging in deliberations with others, and to perform one's citizenship role is an existential recognition that there are others with whom one engages and who might share one's political, social and economic aspirations. So, it seems to us as if democratic citizenship education is a legitimate practice according to which people can talk with one another and simultaneously recognise one another's commonalities and differences. Together, people can enact their responsibilities towards society and the environment. At face value then, there seems to be nothing pernicious about democratic citizenship education.

However, engaging iteratively with others on the basis of exercising one's rights and responsibilities in an atmosphere of coexistence and co-belonging does not necessarily imply that *all* others would be involved. People engaged in enacting democratic citizenship education only do so on account of them sharing a particular space, namely the nation-state. Moving beyond the borders of a nation-state nullifies any act of democratic citizenship education. And this is where cosmopolitan education seems to emerge as a viable sociopolitical theory of human interaction. To be a cosmopolitan is not just a matter of being a citizen of the world in the narrow sense used by the Greek cynic, Diogenes. Rather, being a cosmopolitan implies that one is engaged with all others in the world unconstrained by political borders. In other words, a cosmopolitan being is a stranger to none. Such a view of cosmopolitanism resonates with promoting democratic and peaceful relations with others (Held, 2003). Not being a stranger to others implies a willingness to engage with them and encounter others' ways of living (Waldron, 2000). Yet, not being a stranger to others also implies that one wants to be known by others and to be interested in their humanity (Nussbaum, 2000). In a way, the kind of cosmopolitan education we advance draws eclectically on human encounters to promote peaceful, democratic engagement accompanied by a recognition of others' own cultural and humane ways of being. If such a view of cosmopolitanism is at play, there is always the possibility to be open to new ways and interpretations about the world without being disloyal to one's own ways of being (Papastephanou, 2015).

TOWARDS A COSMOPOLITAN COMMUNITY

To be cosmopolitan-minded, states Hansen (2017: 209),

> is to have a sense of home or place in some substantiating form or another. It is also to have a sense of solidarity, a sense of identity, a sense of meaningful connection with others in the world. In brief, to be cosmopolitan-minded is to inhabit the world.

He explains as follows:

> [C]osmopolitanism as I see it points to a dynamic fusion of reflective openness to the new with reflective loyalty to the known. This fusion points to what can be called cosmopolitan-mindedness, -heartedness, and -spiritedness. Moreover, the fusion of openness and loyalty indicates why cosmopolitanism does not constitute a radically new identity that would supplant local or particular identities. Rather, the orientation has to do with how one perceives, holds, and expresses one's identity. It involves developing a dynamic relation – a living relation – with the values that guide one's life and that of one's community. In this relation, people can come to hold and express their identities and values in peaceful, communicative, and yet determined ways. They can experience why reason and criticism are not *ipso facto* acidic of custom and ceremony, but rather can deepen one's organic relation with them. People discover the primordial truth that they are not just created beings but can be creative beings. Thus cosmopolitan-mindedness walks hand-in-hand with a sense of tradition regarding one's commitments. (Hansen, 2017: 210)

What ensues from this description and the introductory comments is that cosmopolitan education can be considered a defensible educational framework according to which human encounters can be enhanced. It advances human relations peacefully and democratically beyond an insistence that one's own cultural norms are more important than others' ways of being. Most poignantly, such a view of cosmopolitan education seems to be interested in cultivating a humane society without being oblivious of one's own ways of being and acting. Instead, one remains reflexively open to the new and simultaneously open to reconstituting one's own norms and values (Hansen, 2011). By far, cosmopolitan education can reorientate all humans – and not just those within a particular nation-state – to the world of policy and practice (Papastephanou, 2015). Thus, it seems as if democratic citizenship education can lay the groundwork for enacting cosmopolitan education that 'is primarily about a responsible, lawful, loving, thoughtful treatment of the whole cosmos' (Papastephanou, 2015: 17).

What are the ramifications of such a view of education for racial, ethnic and gender under-representivity? To begin with, the most obvious implication of the view of cosmopolitan education developed in this chapter is a notion that transcends race, ethnicity and gender. One's race, which in any case is a social construction, cannot and should not determine one's level of deliberative engagement with others. Likewise, one's sense of openness towards others cannot become a pathway to exclude them on the grounds of ethnicity and culture. In fact, cultural differences should become a stimulant for people to want to engage; otherwise, how would others ever become known to one. Second, the view of cosmopolitanism we have argued for seems to be a nexus of unconditional engagement, nullifying any attempt at gender discrimination. Third, under-representivity, although it might be prevalent at times, should not be a precursor for non-recognition of others and otherness because universal hospitality should be extended at all times to all others.

The point about representivity commensurate with cosmopolitanism has something to do with Giorgio Agamben's (1993) formation of a community to which all belong without any condition of belonging. People engaging with one another's commonalities and differences do so on the grounds of no common or shared identity. In this way, unlike democratic citizenship that requires the state for its enactment, people engaging in a shared identity without reference to either identity or difference actually co-belong in a new community or 'new communism, in which nothing is shared except the power and possibility of life itself' (Mills, 2008: 130). Thus, the upshot of engaging as cosmopolitans in community is, in fact, to 'enter into a community without presuppositions and without subjects, into a communication without the incommunicable' (Agamben, 1993: 65). To remain in communication implies that there is always something to talk about and without being prevented from doing so by the incommunicable means that the possibility for communication is always there as long as the new cosmopolitan community 'share nothing except their own being ... in pure communicability and ontological immediacy' (Agamben, 1993: 65). Simply put, a new cosmopolitan community is always in becoming as there can be no predetermined idea of what such a community would look like.

As long as humans remain in communication with their similarities and differences, they would cultivate a community that is not yet in existence from whatever singularities they (humans) share on condition of their co-belonging. Even if such a cosmopolitan community would be under-represented in terms of race, ethnicity and gender – which in today's world seems highly unlikely – such a community would invariably be engendered 'along a line of sparkling alternation on which common nature and singularity, potentiality and act change roles and interpenetrate' (Agamben, 1993: 20). Hence, cosmopolitan education offers a more tenable framework according to which new communities can be cultivated based on no predetermined condition of belonging. Instead, such a community comprises cosmopolitan individuals whose 'singularities form a community without affirming an identity, that humans co-belong without any representable condition of belonging' (Agamben, 1993: 86). In such cases, under-representivity would perhaps not matter as the new coming community would not be constrained by a shared identity as a condition of belonging, but rather, enacted on what is still to come – what Agamben (1993) refers to as a completed humanity. Under-representivity is a shared identity individuals or groups have in common, whereas a cosmopolitan community is one of co-belonging without any condition of belonging. People differ without necessarily having to agree jointly that they differ. The marginalised groups in terms of race, ethnicity and gender form a new community that exists without any prior agreement of belonging to such groups.

By way of example, we shall now examine whether the idea of a cosmopolitan community is possible in Africa. Over the past two decades, there has been much discussion on working towards an African Renaissance and establishing a community of Africans bounded by the notion of *ubuntu*. As articulated elsewhere, *ubuntu* literally means human dignity and interdependence (Waghid, 2020), and it makes sense to talk about an African community constituted by *ubuntu*. Considering Africa's political, social and economic malaises, any aspiration to cultivate an African community in *ubuntu* seems plausible. So, what does *ubuntu* offer the idea of an African community? First, cultivating human dignity and respect happens when people are in association. They learn to act autonomously – that is, to speak their minds without necessarily affronting others in association with them. The African ethic, 'I am because we are', literally *ubuntu*, is a manifestation that humans live together and are dependent on one another; hence, do not show disrespect towards one another.

Such an idea of *ubuntu* resonates with that of a cosmopolitan community in the sense that Africans are obliged to enact their living based on mutual respect and interdependence. This means that 'a person is only a person through other persons' – *Ubuntu ngumuntu ngabanye abantu* (Waghid et al., 2018).

Second, an *ubuntu* community is formed on the basis of people engaging in deliberation with one another (Waghid, 2020). One cannot begin to think of people in community without being touched by acts of deliberation. Deliberative engagement is a way of people getting to connect with one another and finding out how one another conceive of events in the world. If not, people would live in isolation without ever responding to one another, which seems very unlikely. People's desire drives the interrelationship between a cosmopolitan community and *ubuntu* to deliberate – that is, listening to, talking to and talking back to one another (Waghid, 2020).

Third, an *ubuntu* community is cosmopolitan because people are obliged to engage with one another's differences. On the African continent, where people have diverse cultures and languages, it makes sense to talk about *ubuntu* that will bring them (people) in conversation with one another with the intent to share commonalities and differences. It might just be that imagining an African community in diversity bounded by differences would be cultivated without an abandonment of people's civility and public responsibility. Here, decency and public accountability invoke notions of racial, ethnic and gender justice that undermine any form of under-representivity.

Finally, for Africans, generally speaking, the environment and its protection are sacrosanct. Often people are advised by their traditional leaders to spend some time in the mountains or forest away from home to indicate that the natural environment offers sanctity and peace for self-reflection. So, by cultivating an *ubuntu* community, people are advised to return to their environment and, in so doing, develop a sense of inner peace with their surroundings. Consequently, respecting the environment is done as humans cultivate their *ubuntu* community. For Africans, environmental justice thus emerges as an important practice they have to uphold. This idea of environmental justice finds expression in many people's understanding of what it means to build an *ubuntu* community.

In conclusion, cosmopolitanism, more specifically, cosmopolitan education, is inextricably connected to the notion of democratic citizenship education. By implication, the two education concepts do not have to be considered mutually exclusive forms of education. Instead, in a complementary fashion, cosmopolitan education envelops the notion of democratic citizenship on the grounds of autonomy and deliberative engagement being regarded as constitutive of both forms of education. Then, we have shown how the notion of a cosmopolitan community can be enacted in the form of *ubuntu* that brings people in association with mutual respect and human interdependence.

References

Achinstein, Betty, Ogawa, Rodney T., Sexton, Dena, and Freitas, Casia. 2010. 'Retaining teachers of color: A pressing problem and a potential strategy for "hard-to-staff" schools'. *Review of Educational Research* 80, no. 1: 71–107. https://doi.org/10.3102/0034654309355994.

Agamben, Giorgio. 1993. *The Coming Community*. Translated by Michael Hardt. Minneapolis, MN: University of Minnesota Press.

Ahmed, Sara. 2004. 'Declarations of whiteness: The non-performativity of anti-racism'. *Borderlands* 3, no. 2: 104–126.

Ahmed, Sara. 2007. 'A phenomenology of whiteness'. *Feminist Theory* 8, no. 2: 149–168. https://doi.org/10.1177/1464700107078139.

Ahmed, Sara. 2012. *On Being Included: Racism and Diversity in Institutional Life*. Durham: Duke University Press.

Anderson, Nic. 2017. '"You disappointed the Blacks by getting a good mark": Fresh fury over St John's racist teacher's comments'. *The South African*, 7 July 2017. https://www.thesouthafrican.com/you-disappointed-the-blacks-by-getting-a-good-mark-fresh-fury-over-st-johns-racist-teachers-comments/.

Appiah, K. Anthony. 1994. 'Race, culture, identity: Misunderstood connections'. *The Tanner Lectures on Human Values*, 27–28 October 1994. University of California at San Diego.

Appiah, K. Anthony. 2015. 'Race in the modern world: The problem of the color line'. *Foreign Affairs* 94, no. 2: 1–8.

Badat, M. Saleem. 1999. *Black Student Politics, Higher Education and Apartheid from SASO to SANSCO, 1968–1990*. Pretoria: Human Sciences Research Council.

Banks, James A. 2008. 'Diversity, group identity, and citizenship education in a global age'. *Educational Researcher* 37, no. 3: 129–139. https://doi.org/10.3102/0013189X08317501.

Bauböck, Rainer. 2018. 'Democratic inclusion: A pluralist theory of citizenship'. In *Democratic Inclusion: In Dialogue*, edited by Rainer Bauböck, 1–102. Manchester: Manchester University Press.

Benhabib, Seyla. 1994. 'The generalised and the concrete other'. In *Feminism as Critique: Essays on the Politics of Gender in Late-Capitalist Society*, edited by Seyla Benhabib and Drucilla Cornell, 77–95. Cambridge: Polity Press.

Benhabib, Seyla. 2002. *The Claims of Culture: Equality and Diversity in the Global Era*. Princeton: Princeton University Press.

Benhabib, Seyla. 2004a. *The Rights of Others: Aliens, Citizens and Residents*. Cambridge: Cambridge University Press.

Benhabib, Seyla. 2004b. 'The rights of others. Aliens, residents and citizens'. Conference on 'Migrants, Nations and Citizenship', CRASSH, 5–7 July 2004.

Benhabib, Seyla. 2005. 'Borders, boundaries, and citizenship'. *Political Science and Politics* 38, no. 4: 673–677. https://doi.org/10.1017/S1049096505050328.

Benhabib, Seyla. 2007. 'Democratic exclusions and democratic iterations: Dilemmas of "just membership" and prospects of cosmopolitan federalism'. *European Journal of Political Theory* 6, no. 4: 445–462. https://doi.org/10.1177/1474885107080650.

Benhabib, Seyla. 2011. *Dignity in Adversity: Human Rights in Troubled Times*. Cambridge: Policy Press.

Benhabib, Seyla and Cornell, Drucilla. (Eds.). 1994. *Feminism as Critique: Essays on the Politics of Gender in Late-Capitalist Society*. Cambridge: Polity Press.

Bernstein, Sara. 2020. 'The metaphysics of intersectionality'. *Philosophical Studies* 177: 321–335. https://doi.org/10.1007/s11098-019-01394-x.

Biesta, Gert, Lawy, Robert, and Kelly, Narcie. 2009. 'Understanding young people's citizenship learning in everyday life: The role of contexts, relationships and dispositions'. *Education, Citizenship and Social Justice* 4, no. 1: 5–24. https://doi.org/10.1177/1746197908099374.

Blasdel, Alex. 2018. 'Is white America ready to confront its racism? Philosopher George Yancy says we need a "crisis"'. Accessed 23 March 2021. https://www.theguardian.com/world/2018/apr/24/george-yancy-dear-white-america-philosopher-confront-racism.

Bosniak, Linda. 2006. *The Citizen and the Alien: Dilemmas of Contemporary Membership*. New Jersey: Princeton University Press.

Bush, Tony and Gamage, David T. 2001. 'Models of self-governance in schools: Australia and the United Kingdom'. *International Journal of Education Management* 15, no. 1: 39–44. 10.1108/09513540110380604.

Butler, Judith. 1999. *Gender Trouble: Feminism and the Subversion of Identity*. New York: Routledge.

Celis, Karen. 2013. 'Representativity in times of diversity: The political representation of women'. *Women's Studies International Forum* 41, no. 3: 179–186. https://doi.org/10.1016/j.wsif.2013.07.007.

Cooke, Miriam, Ahmad, Fawzia, Badran, Margot, Moallem, Minoo and Zine, Jasmin. 2008. 'Roundtable discussion: Deploying the muslimwoman'. *Journal of Feminist Studies in Religion* 24, no. 1: 91–99.

Cornell, Drucilla. 1992. *The Philosophy of the Limit*. New York and London: Routledge.

Cornell, Stephen, and Hartmann, Douglas. 1998. *Ethnicity and Race: Making Identities in a Changing World*. Thousand Oaks, CA: Pine Forge Press.

Crenshaw, Kimberle. 1989. 'Demarginalizing the intersection of race and sex: A black feminist critique of antidiscrimination doctrine, feminist theory and antiracist politics'. *University of Chicago Legal Forum* 1, no. 8: 139–167.
Crick, Nathan A. 2016. 'Post-structuralism'. Oxford Research Encyclopedia of Communication. Accessed 23 March 2021. https://oxfordre.com/communication/view/10.1093/acrefore/9780190228613.001.0001/acrefore-9780190228613-e-49.
Davids, Nuraan. 2019. 'You are not like us: On teacher exclusion, imagination, and disrupting perception'. *Journal of Philosophy of Education* 53, no. 1: 165–179. https://doi.org/10.1111/1467-9752.12321.
Davids, Nuraan, and Waghid, Yusef. 2015. 'The invisible silence of race: On exploring some experiences of minority group teachers at South African schools'. *Power and Education* 7, no. 2: 155–168. https://doi.org/10.1177/1757743815586518.
Davids, Nuraan, and Waghid, Yusef. 2019. *Democratic Education and Muslim Philosophy: Interfacing Muslim and Communitarian Thought*. New York and London: Palgrave-MacMillan.
De Haan, Arjan. 2000. 'Debates on social exclusion in the south: What have they contributed to our understanding of deprivation?' Rutland: Uppingham Conference, 11 December 2000.
Delors, Jacques, Al Mufti, In'am, Amagi, Isao, Carneiro, Roberto, Chung, Fay, Geremek, Bronislaw, Gorham, William, Kornhauser, Aleksandra, Manley, Michael, Padron, Quero, Marisela, Savane, Marie-Angélique, Singh, Karan, Stavenhagen, Rudolfo, Won Suhr, Myong, and Nanzhao, Zhou. 1996. 'Learning: The treasure within'. Report to UNESCO of the International Commission for the Twenty-first century. Paris: UNESCO.
Department of Education (DoE). 1996a. *South African Schools Act of 1996*. Pretoria: Government Printer.
Department of Education (DoE). 1996b. *Education White Paper 2: The Organisation, Governance and Funding of Schools*. Pretoria: Department of Education.
Department of Education (DoE). 1998. *National Norms and Standards for School Funding*. Pretoria: Government Printers.
Department of Education (DoE). 2004. *The Ministerial Review Committee on School Governance*. Pretoria: Government Printers.
Derrida, Jacques. 2004. *Eyes of the University: Right to Philosophy 2*. Translated by Jan Plug and others. Stanford, CA: Stanford University Press.
Dewey, John. 1925. *Democracy and Education: An Introduction to the Philosophy of Education*. New York: The MacMillan Company.
Erasmus, Zimitri. 2001. 'Introduction: Re-imagining coloured identities in post-apartheid South Africa'. In *Coloured by History, Shaped by Place: New Perspectives on Coloured Identities in Cape Town*, edited by Erasmus Zimitri, 13–28. Cape Town: Kwela Books.
Erasmus, Zimitri. 2017. *Race Otherwise, Forging a New Humanism for South Africa*. Johannesburg: Wits University Press.
Ferri, Beth A., and Connor, David J. 2005. 'Tools of exclusion: Race, disability, and (re)segregated education'. *Teachers College Record* 107, no. 3: 453–474. 10.1111/j.1467-9620.2005.00483.x.

Fine, Michelle. 2002. '2001 Carolyn Sherif Award Address: The presence of an absence'. *Psychology of Women Quarterly* 26, no. 1: 25–35. https://doi.org/10.1111/1471-6402.00039.

Fraser, Nancy. 1990. 'Rethinking the public sphere: A contribution to the critique of actually existing democracy'. *Social Text* no. 25/26: 56–80. https://doi.org/10.2307/466240.

Fraser, Nancy. 1994. 'What's critical about critical theory?' In *Feminism as Critique*, edited by Seyla Benhabib and Drucilla Cornell, 31–55. Cambridge: Polity Press.

Friedman, Marilyn. 2005. *Women and Citizenship*. Oxford: Oxford University Press.

Giroux, Henry A. 1997. 'White squall: Resistance and the pedagogy of whiteness'. *Cultural Studies* 11, no. 3: 376–389. https://doi.org/10.1080/095023897335664

Golnaraghi, Golnaz, and Dye, Kelly. 2016. 'Discourses of contradiction: A postcolonial analysis of Muslim women and the veil'. *International Journal of Cross Cultural Management* 16, no. 2: 137–152. https://doi.org/10.1177/1470595816660118.

Goodin, Robert E. 1996. 'Inclusion and exclusion'. *European Journal of Sociology* 37, no. 2: 343–371.

Gracia, Jorge E. (Ed.) 2007. *Race or Ethnicity? On Black and Latino Identity*. Ithaca: Cornell University Press.

Graham, Linda J. 2006. 'Caught in the net: A Foucaultian interrogation of the incidental effects of limited notions of "inclusion"'. *International Journal of Inclusive Education* 10, no. 1: 3–24. https://doi.org/10.1080/13603110500173217.

Graham, Linda J., and Slee, Roger. 2008. 'An illusory interiority: Interrogating the discourse/s of inclusion'. *Educational Philosophy and Theory* 40, no. 2: 277–293. https://doi.org/10.1111/j.1469-5812.2007.00331.x.

Gutmann, Amy. 1999. *Democratic Education*. New York: John Wiley & Sons.

Gutmann, Amy. 2003. *Identity in Democracy*. Princeton and Oxford: Princeton University Press.

Habermas, Jürgen. 1984. *The Theory of Communicative Action: Reason and the Rationalization of Society*. Translated by T. McCarthy. Cambridge: Polity Press.

Habermas, Jürgen, Lennox, Sara, and Lennox, Frank. 1974. 'The public sphere: An encyclopedia article (1964)'. *New German Critique* no. 3: 49–55. https://doi.org/10.2307/487737.

Hansen, David T. 2011. *The Teacher and the World: A Study of Cosmopolitanism as Education*. New York: Routledge.

Hansen, David T. 2017. 'Cosmopolitanism as education: A philosophy for educators in our time'. *Religious Education* 112, no. 3: 207–216. https://doi.org/10.1080/00344087.2017.1308180.

Haslanger, Sally. (2014). 'Race, intersectionality, and method: A reply to critics'. *Philosophical Studies* 171, no. 1: 109–119.

Held, David. 2003. 'Cosmopolitanism: Globalisation tamed?' *Review of International Studies* 29, no 4: 465–480. https://doi.org/10.10171S0260210503004650.

Honneth, Axel, and Ranciere, Jacques. 2016. *Recognition or Disagreement*. Edited by Katia Genel and Jean-Philippe Deranty. New York: Columbia University Press.

Ingersoll, Richard, May, Henry, and Collins, Gregory. 2019. 'Recruitment, employment, retention and the minority teacher shortage'. *Education Policy Analysis Archives* 27, no. 37, 1–37. https://doi.org/10.14507/epaa.27.3714.

Jackson, Liz. 2019. 'The smiling philosopher: Emotional labor, gender, and harassment in conference spaces'. *Educational Philosophy and Theory* 51, no. 7: 693–701. https://doi.org/10.1080/00131857.2017.1343112.

Jackson, Sherman, A. 2005. *Islam and the Blackamerican: Looking toward the Third Resurrection.* New York: Oxford University Press.

Jansen, Jonathan D. 2007. 'Learning and leading in a globalized world: The lessons from South Africa'. In *Handbook of Teacher Education: Globalization, Standards and Professionalism in Times of Change*, edited by Tony Townsend and Richard Bates, 25–40. Dordrecht: Springer.

Joseph, Suad. 1996. 'Gender and citizenship in Middle Eastern states'. *Middle East Report*, no. 198: 4–10. https://doi.org/10.2307/3012867.

Karlsson Jenni. 2002. 'The role of democratic governing bodies in South African schools'. *Comparative Education* 38, no. 3: 327–336. https://doi.org/10.1080/0305006022000014188.

Khiabany, Gholam, and Williamson, Milly. 2008. 'Veiled bodies – naked racism: culture, politics and race in the Sun'. *Race & Class* 50, no. 2: 69–88. https://doi.org/10.1177/0306396808096394.

Kirmani, Nida. 2009. 'Deconstructing and reconstructing "Muslim women" through women's Narratives'. *Journal of Gender Studies* 18, no. 1: 47–62. https://doi.org/10.1080/09589230802584253.

Kohli, Rita, and Pizarro, M. 2016. 'Fighting to educate our own: Teachers of color, relational accountability, and the struggle for racial justice'. *Equity & Excellence in Education* 49, no. 1: 72–84. 10.1080/10665684.2015.1121457.

Kroløkke, Charlotte, and Sørenson, Anne Scott. 2006. *Gender Communication Theories and Analyses: From Silence to Performance.* Thousand Oaks, CA: Sage.

Kymlicka, Will. 1995. *Multicultural Citizenship: A Liberal Theory of Minority Rights.* Oxford: Oxford University Press.

Kymlicka, Will, and Donaldson, Sue. 2018. 'Metics, members and citizens'. In *Democratic Inclusion: In dialogue*, edited by Rainer Bauböck, 160–182. Manchester: Manchester University Press.

Leonardo, Zeus. 2009. *Race, Whiteness and Education.* New York: Routledge.

Levinson, Meira L. 2010. 'The civic empowerment gap: Defining the problem and locating solutions'. In *Handbook of Research on Civic Engagement*, edited by Lonnie Sherrod, Judith Torney-Purta, and Constance A. Flanagan, 331–361. Hoboken, NJ: John Wiley & Sons.

Locke, John. 2003. *Two Treatises of Government and A Letter Concerning Toleration.* London: Yale University Press.

MacKinnon, Catherine A. 1983. 'Feminism, Marxism, method, and the state: Toward feminist jurisprudence'. *Signs* 8, no. 4: 635–658.

Makhetha, Tankiso. 2017. 'School racism row: Parents don't want a black principal'. *IOL*, 25 July. https://www.iol.co.za/news/south-africa/gauteng/school-racism-row-parentsdont-want-a-black-principal-10458915.

Marshall, T. H., and Bottomore, Tom. 1950. *Citizenship and Social Class*. Cambridge: Cambridge University Press.

Martin, Joan M. 2000. *More than Chains and Toil: A Christian Work Ethic of Enslaved Women*. Louisville, KY: Westminster John Knox Press.

Masschelein, Jan, and Simons, Maarten. 2013. *In Defense of the School: A Public Issue*. Translated by J. McMartin. Leuven: E-ducation, Culture & Society Publishers.

May, Todd. 2009. 'Democracy is where we make it: The relevance of Jacques Rancière'. *Symposium: Canadian Journal of Continental Philosophy* 13, no. 1: 3–31.

McClain, Linda C., and Grossman, Joanna L. (Eds.). 2009. *Gender Equality: Dimensions of Women's Equal Citizenship*. Cambridge: Cambridge University Press.

McKinney, Carolyn. 2017. *Language and Power in Post-Colonial Schooling: Ideologies in Practice*. New York: Routledge.

McLaughlin, T.H. 1992. 'Citizenship, diversity, and education: A philosophical perspective'. *Journal of Moral Education* 21, no. 3: 235–250. https://doi.org/10.1080/0305724920210307.

Mendieta, Eduardo. 2008. 'Identities: Postcolonial and global'. In *Identities: Race, Class, Gender, and Nationality*, edited by Linda M. Alcoff, and Eduardo Mendieta, 407–416. Oxford: Blackwell.

Miles, Robert. 2000. 'Apropos the idea of "race" … again'. In *Theories of Race and Racism: A Reader*, edited by Les Back and John Solomos, 125–143. New York: Routledge.

Mills, Charles W. 1998. *Blackness Visible: Essays on Philosophy and Race*. Ithaca: Cornell University Press.

Mills, Catherine. 2008. *The Philosophy of Agamben*. Stocksfield, UK: Acumen.

Moorosi, Pontso. 2010. 'South African female principals' career paths: Understanding the gender gap in secondary school management'. *Educational Management Administration & Leadership* 38, 5: 547–562. https://doi.org/10.1177/1741143210373741.

Nussbaum, Martha C. 2000. *Cultivating Humanity: A Classical Defense of Reform in Liberal Education*. Cambridge, MA: Harvard University Press.

Okin, Susan M. 1989. *Justice, Gender and the Family*. New York: Basic Books Inc. Publishers

Owen, David S. 2007. 'Towards a Critical Theory of Whiteness'. *Philosophy & Social Criticism* 33, no. 2: 203–222. https://doi.org/10.1177/0191453707074139.

Papastephanou, Marianna. 2015. *Thinking Differently about Cosmopolitanism: Theory, Eccentricity, and the Globalised World*. Boulder and London: Paradigm Publishers.

Pashby, Karen. 2008. 'Demands on and of citizenship and schooling: "Belonging" and "diversity" in the global imperative'. In *Citizenship Education in the Era of Globalisation: Candian Perspectives*, edited by Michael O'Sullivan and Karen Pashby, 9–26. Rotterdam/Tapei: Sense Publishers.

Pateman, Carole. 1989. *The Disorder of Women: Democracy, Feminism, and Political Theory*. Stanford: Stanford University Press.

Peters, Michael A. 2015. 'Why is my curriculum white?' *Educational Philosophy and Theory* 47 no. 7: 641–646. https://doi.org/10.1080/00131857.2015.1037227.
Peters, Michael A. 2019. 'Interview with George Yancy, African-American philosopher of critical philosophy of race'. *Educational Philosophy and Theory* 51, no. 7: 663–669. https://doi.org/10.1080/00131857.2018.1498214.
Peters, Michael A., and Besley, Tina A. C. 2014. 'Social exclusion/inclusion: Foucault's analytics of exclusion, the political ecology of social inclusion and the legitimation of inclusive education'. *Open Review of Educational Research* 1, no. 1: 99–115. https://doi.org/10.1080/23265507.2014.972439.
Peters, Michael A., and Besley, Tina. 2017. 'Poststructuralism and education: Antifoundationalism, the will to power and the critique of the philosophy of the subject'. In *Reader in Philosophy of education*, edited by Philip Higgs and Yusef Waghid. Cape Town: Juta & Company.
Petzen, Jennifer. 2012. 'Contesting Europe: A call for an anti-modern sexual politics'. *European Journal of Women's Studies* 19, no. 1: 97–114. https://doi.org/10.1177/1350506811426390.
Pitkin, H. 1967. *The Concept of Representation*. Berkeley: University of California Press.
Pitkin, Hanna F. 2004. 'Representation and democracy: Uneasy alliance'. *Scandinavian Political Studies* 27, no. 3: 335–342.
Rancière, Jacques. 1991. *The Ignorant School Master: Five Lessons in Intellectual Emancipation.* Translated by Kristin Ross. Stanford: Stanford University Press.
Rancière, Jacques. 1999. *Disagreement: Politics and Philosophy.* Translated by Julie Rose. Minneapolis: University of Minnesota Press.
Rancière, Jacques. 2002. *Afterword. The Philosopher and His Poor.* Translated by John Drury, Corinne Oster and Andrew Parker. Durham, NC: Duke University Press.
Ranciére, Jacques. 2016. 'The method of equality: Politics and poetics'. In *Recognition or Disagreement: A Critical Encounter on the Politics of Freedom, Equality, and Identity*, edited by Katia Genel, and Jean-Philippe Deranty, 133–155. New York: Columbia University Press.
Rancière, Jacques. 2017. 'Critical questions on the theory of recognition'. In *Recognition and Disagreement: A Critical Encounter on the Politics of Freedom, Equality and Identity*, edited by Katia Genel and Jean-Philippe Deranty, 83–95. New York: Columbia University Press.
Rawls, John. 1971. *A Theory of Justice*. Harvard: Harvard University Press.
Riley, Denise. 1987. 'Does a sex have a history? Women and feminism'. *New Formations* 1: 35–45.
Rorty, Richard. 1979. *Philosophy and the Mirror of Nature*. Princeton, NJ: Princeton University Press.
Ruitenberg, Claudia. 2008. 'What if democracy really matters'. *Journal of Educational Controversy* 3, no. 1: Article 11.
Ruitenberg, Claudia. 2015. 'The practice of equality: A critical understanding of democratic citizenship education'. *Democracy & Education* 23, no. 1: Article 2.
Ryle, Gilbert. 2007. *The Concept of Mind: 60th Anniversary Edition*. London and New York: Routledge.

Simelane, Bheki C. 2017. 'Another Gauteng School Embroiled in a Principal Appointment Row'. *Daily Maverick*, December 5. https://www.dailymaverick.co.za/article/2017-12-05-another-gauteng-school-embroiled-in-a-principal-appointment-row/#.WsoO4ohuZPY.

Soudien, Crain. 2013. '"Race" and its contemporary confusions: Towards a re-statement'. *Journal of Social and Political Theory* 60, no. 136: 15–37. https://doi.org/10.3167/TH.2013.6013603.

Soudien, Crain, and Sayed, Yusef. 2004. 'A new racial state? Exclusion and inclusion in education policy and practice in South Africa'. *Perspectives in Education* 22, no. 4: 101–115.

Stiker, Henry-Jacques. 1999. *A History of Disability*. Ann Arbour: Michigan University Press.

Taylor, Charles. 1994. *Multiculturalism: Examining the Politics of Recognition*. Princeton: Princeton University Press.

Trepagnier, Barbara. 2006. *Silent Racism: How Well-Meaning White People Perpetuate the Racial Divide*. Boulder/London: Paradigm Publishers.

Valdez, Zulema, and Golash-Boza, Tanya. 2017. 'Towards an intersectionality of race and ethnicity'. *Ethnic and Racial Studies* 40, no. 13: 2256–2261. https://doi.org/10.1080/01419870.2017.1344277.

Van Wyk, Noleen. 2007. 'The rights and roles of parents on school governing bodies in South Africa'. *International Journal about Parents in Education* 1, no. 0: 132–139.

Waghid, Yusef. 2011. 'Critical Islamic pedagogy: Possibilities for cultivating democratic citizenship and cosmopolitanism in Muslim schools'. In *Muslim Schools and Education in Europe and South Africa, Religionen im Dialog,* edited by A. Tayob, I. Niehaus, and W. Weisse, 27–38. Berlin: Waxmann.

Waghid, Yusef. 2019. *Towards a Philosophy of Caring in Higher Education: Pedagogy and Nuances of Care*. New York: Palgrave-MacMillan.

Waghid, Yusef. 2020. 'Towards and *ubuntu* philosophy of higher education'. *Studies in Philosophy and Education*. https://doi.org/10.1007/s11217-020-09709-w.

Waghid, Yusef, Waghid, Faiq, and Waghid, Zayd. 2018. *Rupturing African Philosophy on Teaching and Learning: Ubuntu Justice and Education*. New York: Palgrave-MacMillan.

Waghid, Yusef, and Davids, Nuraan. (Eds.). 2018. *African Democratic Citizenship Education Revisited*. New York: Palgrave-MacMillan.

Waghid, Yusef, Davids, Nuraan, Mathebula, Thokozani, Terblanche, Judith, Higgs, Philip, Shawa, Lester, Manthalu, Chikumbutso H., Waghid, Zayd, Ngwenya, Celiwe, Divala, Joseph, Waghid, Faiq, Peters, Michael A, and Tesar, Marek. 2020. 'Philosophy of education in a new key: Cultivating a living philosophy of education to overcome coloniality and violence in African Universities'. *Educational Philosophy and Theory*. https://doi.org/10.1080/00131857.2020.179371.

Waldron, Jeremy. 2000. 'What is cosmopolitan?' *Journal of Political Philosophy* 8, no. 2: 227–243. https://doi.org/10.1111/1467-9760.00100.

Walker, Melanie. 2005. 'Rainbow nation or new racism? Theorizing race and identity formation in South African higher education'. *Race Ethnicity and Education* 8, no. 2: 129–146. https://doi.org/10.1080/13613320500110501.

Walzer, Michael. 1993. 'Exclusion, injustice and the democratic state'. *Dissent* 40, no. 2: 55–64.

White, Patricia. 1999. 'Gratitude, citizenship and education'. *Studies in Philosophy and Education* 18, no. 1–2: 43–52. https://doi.org/10.1023/A:1005183220317.

Wright, Michelle M. 2015. *Physics of Blackness: Beyond the Middle Passage Epistemology*. Minneapolis: University of Minnesota Press.

Yancy, George. 2005. 'Whiteness and the return of the black body'. *The Journal of Speculative Philosophy* 19, no. 4: 215–241.

Yancy, George. 2008. *Black Bodies, White Gazes: The Continuing Significance of Race*. Lanham: Rowman & Littlefield Publishers, Inc.

Yancy, George. 2012. *Look, a White! Philosophical Essays on Whiteness*. Philadelphia: Temple University Press.

Yancy, George, and Del Guadalupe Davidson, Maria. 2016. 'Thinking about race, history, and identity: An interview with George Yancy'. *The Western Journal of Black Studies* 40, no. 1, 3–13.

Young, Iris M. 1989. 'Polity and group difference: A critique of the ideal of universal citizenship'. *Ethics* 99, no. 2: 250–274.

Young, Iris Marion. 2000. *Inclusion and Democracy*. Oxford: Oxford University Press.

Yuval-Davis, Nira. 1991. 'The citizenship debate: Women, ethnic processes and the state'. *Feminist Review* 39: 58–68.

Yuval-Davis, Nira. 1997. 'Women, citizenship and difference'. *Feminist Review* 57: 4–27.

Yuval-Davis, Nira. 2006. 'Intersectionality and Feminist Politics'. *European Journal of Women's Studies* 13, no. 3, 193–209.

Yuval-Davis, Nira. 2011. *The Politics of Belonging: Intersectional Contestations*. Washington, DC: Sage Publications.

Zack, Naomi. 2017. *Philosophy of Race: An Introduction*. New York: Palgrave MacMillan.

Index

academics, xxv, 23, 32, 33, 93; exchange, 8; experiences, 79; philosophy, xxii
activism, 17, 49, 62
African, 31; community, 104, 105; continent, ix, 105; countries, 20, 79; ethic, 104; nation-state, 20; philosophy of education, 31, 117; Renaissance, 104; societies, 32
apartheid, 18, 26, 31, 32, 62, 63, 71, 75, 76, 82, 93–95; oppression, 82; post-, 19, 62, 69, 79, 81, 83

belonging, xxiii, xxvii, xxviii, 13, 14, 18, 21, 24, 37, 52, 54, 55, 60, 92–94; co-, 98, 99, 101, 104; concept of, 52, 93; condition of, 103; notions of, 89; sense of, xxvi, xxvii, xxviii, 44, 52–55, 60, 89, 90, 92, 94
binary, 28, 91; black/white, 28; construction, xxvii, 67; gender, 47, 55; of inclusion/exclusion, 91; masculine/feminine, 46, 53
black: academics, 30; bodies, 28–29; educational institutions, 32; teacher, 33, 80–83, 87, 92; women, xviii, 35, 36, 38, 39, 43
blackness, xxiv, xxv, 23, 28, 35, 37, 58; constructions of, 34

Christian: ethos, 19; prayers, 19
citizen, 3, 4, 6, 17, 48; democratic, 61; in liberal democracies, xxiv, 13
citizenship, xix, xxii, xxiii, xxiv, xxv, xxvi, xxvii, xxviii, 2–4, 6, 13–17, 20, 21, 37, 40, 44, 45, 48–52, 54, 55, 58, 61, 64, 73, 89, 96, 97, 99, 101; activities of, 50; communitarian interpretation of, xxvi, 45; conceptions of, xxiv, 13, 14, 16, 55; concept of, 14, 48; condition of, 99; conduct of, 15; definitions of, 48; democratic, 87; discussion on, 14; dynamic notion of, 51; education, 54; equal, 49; experiences of, xviii; form of, 73; forms of, xxii, xxvi, 18, 45, 53; framework of, 16; function of, 4; gendered, 48–50; learning, xix; liberal conceptions of, xxiii, 13; notions of, 18, 73; oppositional, xxvi, 45; parts of, 14; peripheral, 17, 22, 49; practices of, 49; project, 27; public realm of, xxvi, 45, 51; public sphere of, 38; purposes of, 3; responsibilities, 54; revitalized, 51; rights, 48, 49; status of, 16, 50; stratified, 27; teaching of, xix; universal, 50; universalist conceptions of, xxvi, 50

citizenship education, xxiii, xxiv, xxvii, 13, 15, 17, 20, 44, 54, 55, 58, 60, 61, 64, 89, 95–97, 99, 101; democratic, 97; realm of, xxvi
civic: action, 16; institutions, 15; republican traditions, 48; rights, xxiii, 13
civil, 48; rights of women, 49; society, 9
class: constructions of, xvii; intersections of, 47; modalities, 46
cognitive: capacities, 3; disabilities, 3, 4; frameworks, 30
colonial: orders, xii; powers, x
colonialism, x; enslavements of, 18
coloniality, x; consensus of, xii; foundations of, xii
coloured, 18, 26, 27, 79–81; school, 83
communities, xiii, xvii, xix, xxiii, xxiv, xxviii, 4, 10, 13, 16, 17, 49, 70, 89, 104; democratic, xiii, xiv, xv; impoverished, 83
constitutional: commitment, 10; democracy, 27; end of apartheid, 63; rights, 99
cosmopolitan: being, xxviii, 102; community, 102, 104, 105; education, xxviii, 101–5
cosmopolitanism, 37, 102, 103, 105; view of, xxviii, 102, 103
critical: analysis, xi, xiv, xxvi; consciousness, xi, 73; race theory, xxii, xxv, 35; self-consciousness, 15; theory, 73
cultural: backgrounds, 33, 78, 79; configurations of gender, 54; differences, 40, 53, 103; diversity, 37, 78; synchronicity, 33, 78, 79
cultures, x, xi, xii, xiii, xiv, xvii, xx, xxi, 8, 18, 19, 22, 24, 41, 43, 46, 47, 50, 51, 64, 66, 82, 103; constructions of, xvii; diverse, 105; identities of, 92
curriculum, 18; culturally disconnected, 78; national, 19

decoloniality: cultivating, 31; (re) imagine, 32
dehumanisation, xxiv, 23, 25, 27, 82; of apartheid, 24
deliberation, xxiii, 9, 10, 60, 74, 96, 101; acts of, 105; claims of, 60; on democracy, xxiii, 13; democratic, xviii; with one another, 105; paralytic, 74; people's, 60; political, 7; public, 6, 10; rational, 3; unconstraines, 73
deliberative: conversations, 10; democracy, 67; encounters. See deliberative; encounters; engagement, 74, 96, 105. See also deliberative; engagement; freedom, 97; human actions, 5
democracies: liberal, xviii, xxiv, xxvi, xxvii, 13, 15, 17, 18, 27, 40, 45, 67
democracy, ix, x, xiii, xvii, xviii, xix, xx, xxiii, xxvi, 1, 5, 6, 8, 27, 33, 57, 62, 66, 68, 69, 98, 99; as inclusion, ix; South African, 27
democratic: inclusion, x, xii, xiii, xiv, xv, xvii, xix, xx, xxi, xxii, xxiv, 2–4, 7–10, 14, 23, 34; iterations, 9, 10; justice, 10, 98; legitimacy, 3, 10; politics, xxvi, 15, 17, 57; rights, xxvi, 54, 55; rights of women, 54; society, ix, 4, 44, 70
democratic citizenship, xvii, xviii, xix, xxiii, xxiv, xxv, xxvii, xxviii, 3, 13, 19–21, 23, 27, 35, 44, 57, 59, 60, 62, 76, 87, 89, 95–98, 101, 103, 105; contractual, 21; education, xxii, xxiii, xxiv, xxv, xxvii, xxviii, 13, 19–21, 35, 44, 58–60, 62, 87, 89, 95–98, 101, 103
demographic: exclusion, 9; imperative, 78; parity, 33, 78; transformation, 72
desegregation: implementation of, 63
discourse, xxv, 31, 35, 38, 51; antiracist policy, 38; dominant, 52; hegemonic, 40; hegemonies of, 50

discrimination, xxiii, xxiv, xxv, 7, 18, 23, 38, 40, 59; forms of, xxii, 74; gender, 103
dissensus, ix, xxiv, 14, 60, 85–87; constructive, xxvii, 77
diverse: backgrounds, 82, 83; classroom, 87; groups, 34, 81, 83
diversity: of identities, 6
dominance: of a Christian ethos, 19; hegemonic, xx
dominant, x, xi, 96; community, xiii; conceptions of discrimination, 39; ethos, 53, 92; group, 93; orders, xi, xiv; racial group, 70; spaces, xii
domination: forces of, 21; forms of, 86, 87; system of, 85

economic, 4; inequality, 43, 64
education, ix, x, xiv, xv, xix, xx, xxii, xxiii, 6, 13, 15, 16, 18–20, 27, 31, 32, 37, 52–54, 63, 64, 71, 73, 74, 86, 87, 96, 97, 101, 105; cosmopolitan. *See* cosmopolitan education; curriculum, 18; forms of, 105; humanist view of, 96; transformative, xiii; university, 31, 73, 74
educational: achievements, 52; encounters, xxiv, 14, 21, 60, 71, 72, 74–76, 84, 87; experience, xix; framework, 103; injustice, 78; institutions, xxii, 18, 32; policy reforms, 19; settings, xix, xxvii, xxviii, 50, 77, 89; systems, xxv, 23
educative: process, 6, 7; ventures, 9
emancipatory: action, 85; discourse, 86; opportunities, 86, 87
encounters, xix, xxii, xxviii, 14, 20, 21, 26, 71, 72, 74, 86, 94; deliberative, 61; democratic, 62; educational, xxiv, 14, 21, 60, 71, 72, 74–76, 84, 87; exclusion, 94; human, xxv, xxviii, 10, 20, 21, 24, 27, 84, 102, 103; public, 76
engagements, xiii, xxi, 6, 9, 76, 92; classroom, 75; deliberative, 92, 96–98, 103, 105

epistemic: challenge, 41; logics, 25
equal: ability, 65; access, xvii, 62; beings, 20, 22; capacities, 21, 86; citizenship. *See* citizenship; equal; education, 63; encounters, 21; freedom, 98; human relations, xxiv, 14; recognition, xvii, 87; responsibilities, 45; rights, xvii, 16, 18, 27, 45; status, xxv, 16, 45; treatment, 51, 62
equality, x, xi, xii, xiv, xxiv, xxvi, 8, 14, 21, 45, 50, 52, 57–61, 63, 64, 66, 85, 98; civic, 98; gender, xxvi, 45; notion of, xxvii, 21, 57; of intelligence, 58–60, 64, 66; presumptions of, xxv; presuppositions to, 62
ethic: African, 104; communicative, 72
ethical, 74; agents, 98; alterity, 75; form of democratic inclusion, xv; participation, ix; relationships, 75; responsibility, xiii, xxi; rights, xiii, xxi; significance, 76; value systems, 94
ethnic: diversity, 77, 78; exclusions, xxviii, 89; groups, 41, 44; identities, 41; justice, 105
ethnicity, xi, xvii, xxi, xxii, xxiv, xxv, xxvii, 1, 13, 14, 18, 19, 22, 24, 35, 38, 39, 41–44, 46, 50, 53, 64, 66, 80, 82, 92–94, 97, 98, 103, 104; intersections of, 44; representivity, 67
exclusion, xviii, xix, xxii, xxiii, xxiv, xxvi, 1, 4, 5, 9–11, 18, 27, 33, 38, 43, 53, 55, 60, 73, 82, 89–91, 94, 98; (re)construction of, 23; democratic, 9; dyadic relationship with, xxviii
experiences, xix, xxv, 31, 35, 38; academic, 79; of belonging, xviii, 89; of black males, 39; of black women, xviii; cultural, 78; human, 26, 32; life, xix, 33, 72, 78; lived, xv, xviii, xxi, xxiv, xxv, 23, 64, 76; of marginalisation, 80; masculine, 51; of minority identities, xxv, 35; of

privileged group members, 38, 39; of women, 36, 38, 39, 52

female, 46, 47, 55; academics, 52, 53; black, 81; white, 46
feminine, xxvi, 45, 46, 51, 58, 75; binary, 46, 53; body, 46; -emotion, xxvi, 45
feminism, 47; politics of, 54; third-wave, 47
freedom: of speech, 14, 17, 62; of thought, 14

gender, xi, xii, xviii, xxi, xxii, xxiv, xxv, xxvi, xxvii, 1, 13, 16, 22, 33, 35–39, 42, 45–47, 49, 50, 54, 55, 57, 59, 62, 64, 66, 70, 73, 75, 93, 94, 97, 98, 103–5; binary, 45, 55; -blindness, 73; intersections of, 47; justice, 105; representivity, 67
government, 62, 99; democratic, 62

hegemonic: contributions, 31; discourses, 40
hegemonies, xxii, xxvi, 21, 34, 40, 47, 50, 55, 57; invisible, 30
homogeneity, 51; of citizens, 51; sense of, xx
humanity, xxviii, 96, 102, 104; common, 32, 96; distinctive, 7
humans, xxi, 6–11, 20–22, 42, 44, 54, 60, 71, 72, 75, 76, 85, 97, 98, 103–5; actions, xxiii, 1, 5, 9, 21; actions of, 8; agency, 72; beings, xiii, xxvi, 10, 58, 91, 94; deliberative engagement, 97; dialogues, 75; difference, 41; dignity, ix, xiv, 104; encounters, xxv, xxviii, 10, 20, 21, 24, 84, 102, 103; engagement, xxi, 9, 27; experiences, 26, 32; groups, 24; interaction, xxviii, 101; interdependence, ix, xiv, 105; intersubjectivity, 71; liberation, 54; living, 44, 97, 98, 101; relations, xxiv, 14, 20, 44, 53, 76, 86, 97, 101; responsibilities in society, 54; rights, xxiii, 10, 13, 68; as social beings, 3; subjects, 72

identification: gendered, 37; norms of, 93
identities: categories of, xxv, 35; collective, 14, 94; construction, 94; dimensions, xxiii, 13; formation, xxv, 19, 35; intersectional, xxii; Islamic, 92; markers, xxii, 22, 94; minority, xxv, 35; multi-faceted, 93; multiple, 72, 92; multiplicity of, xxv, 35; narratives, 94; sexual, 92; shared, 103, 104; singular, 46
ideological: framework, xi
inclusion, x, xi, xii, xiii, xvii, xviii, xix, xxi, xxii, xxiii, xxiv, xxviii, 1–3, 5, 6, 8, 9, 11, 13, 14, 17–19, 23, 24, 27, 33, 34, 55, 79, 87, 89–92, 94; contextualised nature of, 2; democratic, xix, 9. *See also* democratic; inclusion; external, xviii, 91; of minorities, 8; models of, 91; notions of, xxiv, xxviii, 89, 91
inequalities, 7, 58, 62, 63; experiences of, 64
institutional: culture, 93; desegregation, 79; spaces, 30, 32; whiteness, 30
intelligence, 21, 64, 66, 85; equal, 21, 86, 87; equality of, 58–60, 63, 66
interdependence, 105; human, ix, xiv, 104, 105
intersectional: analysis, 39; dimensions, xxv, 35; experience, xxv, 35, 38; minority identities, xxv, 35, 39
intersectionality, xxv, 35–39

judgements, 60, 61, 64, 92; freedom of, 74
justice, 76, 97; cultivating, 76, 97; democratic, 10, 98; and equity, 79; within the family, 50; social, 19, 54, 83, 86; work towards, 7

knowledge: insider, 34, 78; production, xii, xiii; racialised views of, 81; representation of, 71

learners, xiii, xix, xxvii, xxviii, 19, 33, 34, 63–66, 69, 72, 74, 75, 77, 79–87, 89, 93, 94; black, 64, 79, 80; black scholarship, 64; bodies, 33; demographics, 70, 79, 80; disadvantaged, 80; diverse, 87; equality, 63; experience, xxvii, 77; majority group, 33, 86; migratory patterns of, 79; minority-group, 33, 78, 79, 86; white, 63, 64
learning: notion of, xxviii, 89, 96; principles of, 96
legal: accountability, 21; dimensions, xxiii, 13; end of apartheid, 63; equality, xxvi, 57; rights, xxiii, 13, 16, 49
liberal, 2; conceptions of citizenship, xxiii, 13; democracies, xviii, xxiii, xxiv, xxvi, xxvii, 13, 15–18, 27, 40, 41, 45, 67
liberation: black, xiii. *See also* black liberation; women's, xiii

male: body, 46; perspectives, 47
marginalisation, xx, xxii, 38, 39, 59, 72, 91; experiences of, 80
masculine: ethos, 53; superiority, 75
misrecognition, xviii, 7; misguided, 95; of others, 7
moral: commitment, 10
Muslim: non-, 37; religious extremists, 37; women. *See* Muslim; women

normativity, 18; Anglo-Christian, 18

oppression, x, xii, xiii, xxv, 7, 20, 24, 25, 33, 38–40, 42, 46, 51, 75, 94; forms of, 36, 39
otherness, xxi, 75, 101, 103; forms of, 92; recognition of, xviii

participation, xvii, xix, xxiii, 4, 13–15, 27, 45, 47, 51, 69, 73
participatory, 15, 68; human actions, 5
patriarchal: power, 47; structures, 49, 50

pedagogical: access, 82; authority, 64, 82
people of colour, 16, 17, 29, 42
philosophical: diversity, 37
philosophy of education, 31, 32, 71
pluralism, 72, 96
political: agency, xxvi, 4, 53, 55, 57, 72; borders, xxviii, 102; citizenship, 27, 48, 49; membership, 14; morality, 48, 72; power, 14, 41, 43; representation, 18, 68; rights, xxiii, 13, 48; significance, 25, 76; theory, 47, 48, 101
postcolonial, xx, 62
poststructuralism, xx, xxi, 73
poststructuralist: thought, xx, 73
power: relations, x, xi, xviii, xxi, 46, 70, 91; social ontological, 29; structures of, 33, 54
privilege, xxii, xxv, xxvi, 3, 27, 29, 31, 35, 37, 39, 43, 57, 63, 72, 93
public: accountability, 105; schools, 19, 69, 79, 83; sphere, xvii, xviii, xix, xxi, xxii, xxvi, 1, 30, 38–40, 45, 48, 49, 51–53, 59

race, xi, xii, xvii, xxi, xxii, xxiv, xxv, xxvii, 2, 13, 18, 19, 23–26, 35–44, 46, 47, 50, 63, 64, 66, 70, 76, 79, 80, 82, 92–94, 97, 98, 103, 104; articulation of, 27; intersections of, 44, 47
racial: backgrounds, 78, 79; binaries, 63; categories, xi, xxii, 27, 28; categorisation, 24, 80, 94; discrimination, 36, 76; diversity, 78; economic inequality, 43; ethnicity, 42; exclusions, xxviii, 89; heterogeneity, 70; identities, xviii, 27, 29, 33, 42, 83; inequality, 33, 62; justice, 25, 105; lines, 83, 87; oppression, 24; power, 30; segregation, 32; transformation, 33
racialisation: process of, 44
racialised: groups, 28; perspective, 29; as white, 29

racially: -constructed lines, 26; homogenous, 70; white, 41
racism, xiii, xxii, 25, 27, 33, 37, 38, 43, 64, 72, 78, 81; institutional, 33; silent, 43, 44; structural, 44
racist: attitudes, 44; ideologies, 43; individual, 33; practices, 29, 43; stereotype, 87
recognition, x, xvii, xviii, xxiii, xxvii, xxviii, 3, 7, 13, 14, 18, 25, 26, 54, 58, 60, 62, 83–85, 87; inclusive processes of, xviii, 91
relationships: contractual, xxiii, xxiv, 13, 14, 16, 17, 19–21; dyadic, xviii, xxvi, xxviii, 2, 57, 89; equal, 21, 22
religion, xvii, xxvi, 14, 19, 22, 37, 41, 47, 50, 70, 98, 99
religious: instruction, 19; rights, xxiii, 13
representation, 67, 68, 71; notion of, 76, 84; substantive, 68, 69; under-, xxvii, 50, 67, 71–73, 77
representative, 68–70, 72; democracy, 70; human actions, 5; selves, 75; of the types of communities, 72
representivity: teacher, 77, 86; view of, 84
respect, ix, xiv, xxvii, 17, 75–77, 84, 87, 91, 92, 96–98, 101, 104, 105; inclusive processes of, xviii; mutual, 17
rights, 6, 8, 19, 49, 50, 54; associated, xxiii, 13, 14; citizenship, 48, 49; civic, xxiii, 13; civil, 16; constitutional, 99; cultural, xxiii, 13; democratic, xxvi, 54, 55; equal, xvii, 16, 18, 27, 45; ethical, xxiii, 13; human, xxiii, 10, 13, 16, 68; language, 18; legal, xxiii, 13, 16, 49; liberal, 48; political, xxiii, 13, 48; and responsibilities, xxiii, xxv, xxviii, 13, 72, 101; set of, xxvi, 16, 57; social, xxvi, 13, 14; universalist, 9, 10

school, 34, 50, 63–65, 75, 78, 81, 83, 91, 94
segregation, xxiii, 18, 25, 79, 91; physical, 27
sexism, 35, 38; sum of, xxv
sexuality: constructions of, xvii; identities of, 92; intersections of, 47
social: construction, xxiv, 25, 42, 91, 103; contexts, 60; exclusion, xxviii, 4, 41, 90; groups, 25, 43, 73; hegemonies, 62; inequalities, 21, 62, 64; justice, 19, 54, 83, 86; life, 4, 48, 93; matters, 8, 15, 21; membership, 3, 4; practices, 30, 93; responsibilities, xxvi, 55; rights, 13, 14; spaces, x, 94; transformation, ix; transmission of culture, 42; world, xxv, 20, 22, 29–31, 35, 85
society: part of, xxvi, 57; pluralist, 34; sub-structures of, xxvi, 45, 88
South African: schools, 19, 33, 63, 69, 72, 83; society, 18, 27
students, xxvii, xxviii, 52, 65, 66, 72, 74, 75, 77, 84–86, 89
systemic: racism, 43

teacher: demographics, 33, 80; knowledgeable, 85; minority-group, 86; workforce, 78, 79
teaching: community, xxvii, 77; culturally responsive, 34, 78; practice, 72, 75; universal, 65–66; workforce, 78
teaching and learning, xix, xxv, xxvii, 24, 62, 64, 69, 77, 86, 87; communities, xxvii; discourse, 86, 87
transformation, xiii, xvii, 24, 72, 81
transformative: education. *See* education, transformative; struggles, xiv

ubuntu, ix, xiv, 104; community, 105; form of, 105; idea of, 104 universal, 96; basis for feminism, 46; citizenship, 50; conception of citizenship, xxiv, 16; hospitality, 103; human rights, 68; teaching, 66; values. *See* values; voice, 39; womanhood, 47

values, 7, 29, 93, 102, 103; Calvinist, 19
violence, x, 29, 54

Western: Europe, 25; philosophy, xxii, 31
white, 76; competence, xxv, 24, 81; historically, 80–83, 87; learners, 63, 64; males, xxii, 31; man, 37; people, 27, 28, 43; schools, 33, 80–84, 87; staff, 92; woman, 37
whiteness, xxii, xxiv, xxv, 19, 23, 25, 27–29, 35, 42, 43
womanhood, 37, 48; universal, 47
women, xxvi, 36, 39, 45–47, 54, 75; black, 36, 94. *See also* black, women; bodies of, 40, 48, 54; and citizenship, 48; of colour, 36; Muslim, xviii, 37, 40–41, 92; oppressed, 40; rights of, 48, 49

About the Authors

Nuraan Davids is professor of philosophy of education in the Department of Education Policy Studies, Faculty of Education at Stellenbosch University. Her primary research interests include democratic citizenship education; Islamic philosophy of education; and philosophy of higher education. She is a Co-Editor of the Routledge series, *World Issues in the Philosophy and Theory of Higher Education*; Co-Editor-in-Chief of the *Journal of Education in Muslim Societies*; Associate Editor of the *South African Journal of Higher Education*; Editorial Board Member of *Ethics and Education*. Recent books (with Y. Waghid) include: *Academic Activism in higher education: A living philosophy for social justice* (Springer, 2021); *Teaching, friendship & humanity* (Springer, 2020); *Teachers Matter: Educational Philosophy and Authentic Learning* (Rowman & Littlefield – Lexington Series, 2020).

Yusef Waghid is distinguished professor of philosophy of education in the Department of Education Policy Studies at Stellenbosch University. During his tenure at Stellenbosch University, he has occupied management positions of director, chair, dean and acting dean. He holds three doctorates in the areas of philosophy of education (Western Cape, 1995), education policy studies (2000) and political philosophy (Stellenbosch, 2001).

His research foci include analytical philosophy of education within the genres of democratic citizenship education, African philosophy of education, higher education transformation and religious education and ethics.

He is editor-in-chief of the *South African Journal of Higher Education* and principal editor of the internationally acclaimed journal *Citizenship Teaching and Learning*. Considered by the National Research Foundation (NRF) as an internationally acclaimed scholar, he has 337 research publications, of which 31 are authored books and edited collections. His academic stature is affirmed by a number of research accolades. These include awards from the Education Association of South Africa and the South African Association for Research and Development in Higher Education. In 2011, he was honoured with the prestigious NRF Special Recognition Award 'Champion of Research Capacity Development at Higher Education Institutions in South Africa' in recognition of his influence and significant contribution towards the transformation of the social science community in South Africa. In 2014, he received the 'Education in Africa Award for Outstanding Mentorship to Doctoral Students' from the African Development Association. To date, he has produced twenty-five PhDs in educational philosophy and theory – many of whom currently occupy senior academic positions in the African higher education sector.

www.ingramcontent.com/pod-product-compliance
Lightning Source LLC
Chambersburg PA
CBHW020125010526
44115CB00008B/984